DARE
TO DO
NOTHING

AMY MINTY

PUBLISHED BY TRIMARK PRESS, INC., DEERFIELD BEACH, FLORIDA.

LIBRARY OF CONGRESS CATALOGING-IN-PUBLICATION DATA

DARE TO DO NOTHING
BY AMY MINTY

ISBN: 978-1-943401-88-8
LIBRARY OF CONGRESS CONTROL NUMBER: 2021913382
P. CM.

G-21
10 9 8 7 6 5 4 3 2 1
FIRST EDITION
PRINTED AND BOUND IN THE UNITED STATES OF AMERICA

A PUBLICATION OF TRIMARK PRESS, INC.
1525 NW 3RD STREET, SUITE 10
DEERFIELD BEACH, FL 33442
800.889.0693
WWW.TRIMARKPRESS.COMTA

For my husband Ron, who struggles with doing nothing.

Contents

Author's Note

FOR THOSE OF YOU who are unfamiliar with my writing to date, I have written five novels. However, as the world changes, it appears I am changing along with it. This past year, while we all suffered, I had time to do a little introspection and remember my philosophy on life. So I decided to write this book about it. The result became *Dare To Do Nothing*, which is a tongue-in-cheek look at the importance of not trying too hard in life. In fact, doing as little as possible is the ultimate goal.

Achievements are somewhat overrated, especially since they require such tremendous effort. We only go around once, so what we should focus on is living in the present and having a great time. Using personal examples from my past, I write about various topics which demonstrate how to do less. If we are fixated on pleasure as opposed to self-imposed obligations, we regain control of our lives and can do what is really important – eat, sleep, drink, smoke, and have sex.

This is not a novel. This is reality.

CHAPTER 1

Part 1:

The Concept Of Doing Nothing In Daily Life

Is there anything finer than having nothing to do? No, not really. I will expand on this subject in order to give you a cozy feeling about me. I consider myself to be an expert on the subject of "doing nothing," so you're in good hands. I developed such expertise from many years of fine-tuning my skills. Allow me to elaborate.

"Doing nothing" can't be taken literally, of course. There are better things to do than sit in one spot all day. We have to do *something* to keep ourselves occupied, or more specifically, entertained. The point is, there are simple ways to achieve this state of nirvana without having to exert much effort.

Spare time should be well spent. I'm referring to the precious moments that aren't wrapped up in bullshit, obligatory duties. During this time, only do what you desire. But start small. For instance, if you feel like painting, start by experimenting on a small piece of paper. Don't buy twelve gallons of paint and a sixteen-foot canvas and expect to paint like Picasso.

In life, a normal day consists of roughly fourteen to sixteen waking hours. Half of this time is generally spent working or doing stuff we would prefer not to be doing. That's when "doing nothing" really becomes imperative, because, if we hate what we're doing – wouldn't we rather be doing nothing? When faced with the choice, staring at the wall seems pretty good compared to entering data into a computer for some manager on a power trip who thinks he or she owns us.

As you read through this book, you will understand that "doing nothing" is a talent that everyone can develop with a little practice. I will focus on how to enjoy life while exerting minimal effort. Think of it as a stress-free guide to having fun while still doing less. It does require reading, however, but reading is rather relaxing – especially if you're supposed to be working. Writing a book might seem contradictory to the subject matter of "doing nothing," but writing is just a quiet, introverted activity. Trust me, I know.

I'm sure there has been other documentation written about the subject of "nothing," but I've never been interested enough to actually find out, much less read it. I'm aware that the existing literature on my favorite topic concentrates primarily on philosophical concepts. (I despise reading books in search of answers to questions that nobody knows. Life is confusing enough.) This particular book will be a more practical, hands-on approach.

I'll begin by describing myself. I'll try to be objective. I'm one of those people who should probably be on medication, but no one's ever been able to pin me down long enough to diagnose me. Let's just say I'm a free spirit. I'm easily bored, highly erratic, and unpredictable, yet relatively lazy at the core. My bookshelves are stocked with "get rich quick" books, and the like. I always feel there might be one out there that I haven't read, and that bothers me.

As far as my appearance is concerned, I'm short. I think that's because I never ate anything with calcium growing up as a kid. My mother specialized in cooking potatoes. Baked, broiled, fried, grilled, even thrown directly into an actual fire. As long as they were cooked/burned, no matter how they were prepared, they were considered energy-burning fuel for my sister and me. The only calcium I ever ingested was the occasional melted cheese on "charred" potato skins, and that's if I were seriously lucky! Maybe I ate some other foods with calcium, but I sincerely doubt it. Moving on.

My skin is that pale type that needs to be tricked into tanning. Now I live in South Florida, and the sun teases me year-round. Taunting me with ideas of glistening, golden skin as I apply my 50 sunblock.

I think of myself as athletic, but it takes some convincing for others to agree. (You will soon learn about my rigorous gym regiments dating back some twenty years.)

No one can decide on the color of my eyes, which results in many dull conversations. I'm average looking for the most part, which is super because it gives me a very slippery quality: here one minute, gone the next. Yes!

As far as my background is concerned, I went to high school, (half the time – I made sure I attended just enough days to advance grades) then college (five-year plan). One could even say I achieved a few goals before I became a writer, but the bottom line is for the last twenty-five years, I've focused on doing nothing. And you know what? I've had a great time! Additional experiences will be revealed in bits and pieces throughout the remainder of this book, so prepare yourself.

I consider myself to be pretty smart. Not book smart. Those people are annoying. I classify myself more along the lines of streetwise. If I traveled more outside of the U.S., I would even deem myself worldly. Put it this way: I can't answer most of the questions on *Jeopardy*, but I can analyze the contestants to the point where friends and family start sneaking out of the room so they don't have to listen to me. On the other hand, I'm great at *Wheel of Fortune* and *The Price is Right*. Doing a lot of nothing turns you into a damn good guesser and a fantastic shopper.

The best part about doing nothing is what you notice about other people when you're not so focused on your own ambitions, or lack thereof. In short, you have time to make fun of everyone. People are strange. It's entertaining to dissect them from a distance.

Just so everyone understands what I'm truly all about, I'm going to take you through a two-hour segment of my life doing nothing. I would make it a day example, but you might get bored. No one wants that.

Due to the global pandemic caused by the coronavirus in 2020, I'm choosing a two-hour example from my younger years. This will help to maintain a positive outlook and will not be depressing. I take you back to early 2001, prior to 9/11.

Working nights, I would usually rise around noon. This provided me time to relax before my day kicked into full gear. This particular day, my slightly irritating but *useful* friend, Brian, came over to fix my VCR. Other than buzzing him in and out of my apartment, I did absolutely zero during the twenty minutes he was at my apartment. Well, that's not entirely true; I did compliment his Hugo Boss belt and glanced at him occasionally fiddling with the mechanism. In truth, I gaped at him while he gripped the remote control determinedly in the hopes of reprogramming my channels.

People who know what they're doing tend to look intense and resolute. I never look like that. Naturally, that is. I usually appear blissfully happy because I'm not listening to anyone. Nor do I ever know if I'm doing something correctly. Ignorance *is* bliss, by the way. Brian's face was all scrunched up in exasperation as he pressed multiple buttons angrily. He could have passed as someone who worked at the DMV or the FBI. He also never spoke so it wasn't a super-informative lesson, but as long as he fixed my VCR, I didn't give a shit. The beauty was, I didn't have to do a thing. Come to think of it, I didn't even offer him a drink or coffee, which – almost twenty years later – I now realize was rather rude of me.

Next in my heavy lineup for the day, I sauntered over to the gym. Back then, I liked to walk down Christopher Street in Manhattan. The retail shops on that road totally fit into my mindset because none of them sold anything of real value. The stores specialized in paraphernalia which is only handy in the bedroom, depending on your lifestyle.

The gym for me is the epitome of doing nothing. My entrance normally went unnoticed by the "professional" crew at the desk. They buzzed me in automatically because they understood that my daily arrival was part of their boring day. Sometimes I got a nonchalant "hey" when reaching past them for a towel, but generally, I would slink in and out without so much as a nod.

I eventually found myself staring at the same uniform blue locker. I always went directly to locker number forty-three, which had a broken handle. I'm not sure why I always chose that particular compartment to store my bag, but it was probably because, being broken, it had a ninety-eight percent chance of being unoccupied. Whatever the case, I repeatedly found myself standing in front of its bent exterior. I glanced around like I always did, marking my territory and staring at my reflection in the multitude of mirrors. A whole lot of nothing happens in front of all those mirrors. What a waste. It's never like what you see in the movies.

After getting changed into my hip workout gear, which I can't specifically recall but assume included zebra-striped biking pants, I managed to drag myself up the five flights of stairs to the top floor where they kept the stationary bikes. I'm afraid of elevators, but I use this phobia to my advantage. Climbing the stairs, no matter how slowly, incidentally builds stamina and strong leg muscles.

Being so organized and all, I carried with me the latest paperback bestseller by some guy I'd never heard of, which I knew I'd never wind up reading (it was just for show), and 24 Hour Fitness' small white towel, which was even more unnecessary than the book. Plopping down on one of the bikes, I began my routine of slow peddling, mixed with an occasional straightening of my posture, while I glanced around the room. "Yep, looks the same as it did yesterday," I thought to myself. More nothing set in.

Then suddenly, I blinked twice – the bike's digital clock indicated I'd been peddling for seven minutes. I might have been so bored that I blacked out, but I figured since I was still on the bike and not sweating in the least, I was OK. I shifted my attention to a tan, good-looking trainer, whom I concluded was "training" an older gentleman. It looked to me as if the trainer was holding him up, but I could have been wrong. I'm not always right. Only ninety-eight percent of the time, but whatever.

Truthfully speaking, I respect trainers. If I were to ever actually do anything, I think I would become a trainer because they're just like me, except for being in better shape and twenty times more active. It had to be better than my job at the time, but I'll get into that in a bit.

A few minutes passed, and I heard the trainer say to his gray-haired client, "Hey, you feel dizzy, just take it easy, man. Sit quietly for a second." *Shit, I'd be great at this job! I know how to encourage resting!* I nicknamed the trainer Rick. I figured my odds were pretty good. I labeled his client, Silver, for obvious reasons.

"When's your next appointment, damn it!" Silver roared, but it wasn't a question, obviously. More of a command. And his hair was mostly white, not silver, but I do recall giving him the benefit of the doubt.

"Eight thirty," Rick said. It was roughly 5 p.m. Give or take. I only happened to know the time because Brian had been over, and I glanced at my watch way too many times. *Rick was living the dream. Three and a half hours of doing nothing and getting paid?* I made a mental note to look into this personal training career. It seemed super promising.

"Do you want to catch a bite to eat?" Silver yelled over the shitty gym music and roaring air conditioning. From my position on the bike, you could tell he was starving for food that tasted good and absolutely hated the current diet his wife had put him on – in order to save his life, of course. You can always tell these things when you're sitting on a stationary bike barely moving your legs.

"Sure," Rick said with enthusiasm. The two proceeded to limp out of the room together. My immediate thought was this: Rick automatically adopted his client's mannerisms. It was like watching *General Hospital* from the director's chair on set. It was surprisingly refreshing/suspicious to see two opposites get along so well. I was so darn entertained that I forgot to keep cycling. My bike reminded me of this by blinking obnoxiously, a not-so-subtle cue to keep pedaling.

I looked down at the back cover of my book for the thirteenth time. "Shocking!" "A Superb Read!" "Hooks You Right In!" Damn, I thought. I still had no idea what the book was about, but I'd somehow memorized the accolades from the press.

I persevered. I was almost about to break the twelve-minute mark. I always knew when that was about to happen. For some reason it's a small hurdle of achievement for me. I think it's because I used to be able to run a twelve-minute mile back in my youth. I've since realized it's more satisfying to see I can bike double the mileage in that time – without even trying.

I contemplated glancing over the back cover of the novel I was still hopelessly holding when I was saved by yet another bizarre distraction. An older lady, maybe in her early seventies, was hobbling up the stairs. (Afraid of elevators too, and no doubt looking for Silver, who was off eating pizza with Rick. But she was elegant and classy. I instantly named her Lady Di, peddling slightly faster, nervous and excited at each tap of her cane. I have a vivid imagination, and I was thrilled to be among royalty.

Naturally, feeling my positive momentum (if only temporary) and amazing vibes, Lady Di chose the bike next to mine, ignoring the six others farther away. She perched her cane thoughtfully over the edge of MY bike, still drawn to my empowering energy. I continued to watch her, but was afraid to say anything. She looked serious, as most royals do. This was clearly not her first rodeo. My admiration for this woman, who was probably unaware her husband was palling around with Rick and ignoring his strict diet, began peddling to set the clock on her bike, but get this: she only used her right leg. Lady Di kept her left leg balanced on the bar in the middle of the bike while she set her personalized program like a pro.

I was impressed. It was obviously some physical therapy routine, but the fact that she didn't bother to use her "good" leg was fabulous. Her regal elegance regarding basic mannerisms and tricky maneuvers were noteworthy. Lady Di stared at the television that loomed above us with utter disinterest, peddling slowly with just one leg. After five minutes, I'd dubbed her my personal hero. She made my nothing look like something! She soon got sick of that particular bike. It happens.

Perhaps she thought it was broken.

Lady Di then went from bike to bike, trying them all, each time placing her cane down on the bike to the left of her.

I eventually forced myself to stop staring and glared at myself in the mirror. Twenty-six minutes, 4.2 miles, and 105 calories burned. I had wasted twenty-six minutes burning off the calories of half a Devil Dog.

I walked over to the disturbing, deep blue mats in the corner, forgetting my untouched towel with a shrug, shaking my legs out like a professional athlete. My legs always felt exactly the same after my bike ride, which was a great relief. An injury would simply add one more issue to my hectic schedule.

I extended my legs out in front of me to the best of my

ability, making a big show of it, acting like I knew the definition of agility to anyone that might be watching, and/or cared. Lady Di made her way over to me without invitation. I have a powerful presence, and our mutual respect was obvious. We both seemed to understand the point of doing the least we could at a gym.

Proving my point further, Lady Di laid down on the thick blue mat, perhaps with the idea of a future sit-up in mind. I didn't stay long enough to see if it ever happened. I headed back down the same five flights of stairs to the *super boring* locker room to shower.

Showering took two minutes, as I'd recently decided to have the majority of my hair chopped off. It was kind of a rash decision, but it totally paid off. My haircut was a great addition to my low-maintenance lifestyle. Here's why:

- It required infrequent washing.
- There wasn't enough of it to tangle.
- It was cost efficient.
- Hairbrushes were unnecessary.
- It tended to stay in one place.
- People avoided me, thinking I might have fled a mental institution.
- I no longer had to search my apartment for a hair band.
- It was unaffected by rough sex.
- It was much harder for me to get gum stuck in it.
- It never blocked my vision on a windy day
- People were suddenly forced to look me in the eye.
- I couldn't be told to put my hair up in order to please some corporate prick manager.

Back to the locker room. I told you about the hair for a reason. It explains why my two-inch locks are a snap to fix after a good workout! After wetting my hair under the shower, I waltzed back to locker number forty-three. I glanced around my domain. This was my territory, and I was proud of it.

I dressed leisurely while munching on some caramel corn that I had tucked away in my purse. I also sipped from a lukewarm Yoo-hoo, a well-known super-hydrator used by world-class athletes, which was also in my purse. I then put on some highly regarded Cover Girl makeup purchased from Duane Reade, sprucing up for my big night at work. (Working is just fucking stupid, but we'll get into that shortly.)

Right, so there is a two-hour time slot in the ever-so-exciting life of Amy Minty. I will bring you deeper into the importance of doing nothing as we move forward together.

CHAPTER 1

Part 2:
Doing Nothing At Work

I hate working. I wish I didn't have to. It's bullshit. In 2001, pre-9/11, I was working as a cocktail waitress in what was supposed to be an "elegant" and "charming" champagne lounge. *How glamorous.* Clearly, since they hired me, it wasn't a job that had any real structure or required a tremendous amount of skill.

The job might even sound appealing to someone who has no idea about the service industry. "Champagne Lounge" is just a fancy name for a pretentious bar. For the benefit of this book and stories pertaining to this *particular* work place, I have to give it a fake name. This way I can trash the joint freely and won't be sued immediately, as shockingly, they are still in business. At least as of March 2020.

I'll refer to this horror show establishment as "Flask." That seems appropriate considering the type of clientele it probably still attracts. I will throw myself back in time, present tense, for the sake of the story:

Working at Flask, I mostly keep my cool, but, every once in a while, I find myself running around ungracefully and yelling at everybody. Sometimes I even grab a flashlight and pretend to search the walk-in cooler for a missing bottle of vintage champagne. I eat A LOT of expensive caviar while I wave that flashlight around. (I'm the only employee that cares if we have extra DD batteries in the stock room.) The lounge itself imports fabulous smoked salmon from a colder region in Canada, if that's indeed possible, and it's all cut up in bite-sized pieces, waiting for me to consume them. Strangely, I feel like these culinary geniuses trapped in Flask's basement have prepared these delicacies with me in mind. I know this is truly not the case, but it still feels good to dream. After I pop open a split of bubbly and locate the toast points, I totally forget what I'm supposed to be doing. I'm only focused on the whereabouts of the expensive champagne. I've been swiping the best bottles and selling them Sunday afternoons on Canal Street.

My job truly takes doing nothing to the next level. When I'm not "working" the main floor lounge or upstairs fooling around, I'm actually responsible for remembering customers' orders and making sure they receive it at some point. It's such a hassle, really, but thankfully, I'm not being timed, so I take slow service to new heights. If I'm really lucky, I get a little trainee to boss around while I read my magazine and sip champagne. It just so happens that we're always hiring because people are always quitting. Shocking. If I had any self-worth, I'd quit too, but that would mean finding another job. Hence, I remain at Flask, and at least twice a week, I corrupt a fresh new face, eager to be employed.

Truth be told, I have an *edge* over the newbies because I "helped" open the bar four months ago. My co-workers and I had two days of intensive training. I rolled out of bed and tasted at least a hundred different champagnes and all the food on the menu. I know a good thing when it strikes me over the head. Now, I'm the last remaining soldier from the opening staff. This is only because I live for champagne and caviar, and I'm used to shitty tips. It's not because I'm loyal or anything.

Alright, I've given you enough background information so you can picture me in this rich setting. The only thing I've neglected to explain is that Flask sometimes hosts these god-forsaken private parties that infiltrate all areas of the upstairs lounge. When this happens, I go into hiding. Literally, no one sees me for hours, and I claim to have been passing out hors d'oeuvres the whole time. *Right. As if.*

Allow me to give you a specific example:

I approached Flask around eight p.m., carrying a brown-bag lunch and a semi-automatic. Just kidding. My versatile hair was slicked to my head due to rain, and I felt two days away from an impending cold. I'd been tipped off that I was about to embark on one of those let-the-animals-out-of-the-zoo, free-for-all gatherings. The doorman's expression verified this fact.

I backed away from the front entrance slowly, with a finger to my lips. I then took the sneaky back entrance through the one rough courtyard on Park Avenue, smoked a cigarette, then headed up the fire escape to the second-floor landing.

This bought me time. It took twenty minutes for my "manager," Laurent, to find me. Ha! That's twenty minutes of not being immediately put to work! An accomplishment in itself! I would go into detail describing Laurent, but I can do it in two words: He's French. His first day on the job with me was as a waiter. I hate that word, *waiter*. It's so misleading. It basically implies we will wait on you. What are the chances? Anyway, the next day our general manager quit and the owner, who was also French, told Laurent to come in the following day dressed in a suit and tie and take over. It was a fantastic turn of events. Laurent was like a little nugget of gold you stumble over when you're roaming the desert, barefoot and broke.

I was snacking on a few of the miniature puff pastries arranged on a random silver platter when Laurent tapped me on the shoulder. "Ahhh—Aimeeee. I didn't see you come in! It's so good to see you!" We kissed on both cheeks, as you would do in France or any pretentious environment, really.

"I can't move in here!" I shouted over the crowd.

Laurent looked around and threw up his arms, but he was still smiling, eyes glistening. He knew for certain that this job was better than the French prison he'd just fled. "Yes, just do your best, OK?" And he was off to snort more cocaine while I went to find Carol. Carol was one of my best buddies and Laurent's main squeeze at the time. More importantly, she shared my natural instinct to do nothing. Almost all the employees did, which heightened the laid-back environment and consistently chill vibes.

"Carol," I said, "What's this brainless party about? It looks like a bunch of privileged jerkoffs. Do they all go to NYU? Is anyone older than twenty-one?" We were in our side area and somewhat sheltered from the crowd.

"Fuck knows? But NYU, absolutely."

"What's the party for?"

"Oh, you know . . . blah, blah, blah . . . a benefit for children . . . open bar. I'm just ignoring everyone when they ask for drinks. I say, 'Do I look like the bar? Go to the bar!'"

"Good, so you're not serving anything free. That's my girl," I said, picking a piece of lint off my tight, shiny shirt. I hadn't worn my official uniform in weeks.

"Really, there's like *totally* nothing to do. There's some food we're supposed to be passing out, but I'm just throwing the platters down anywhere I can find space."

"Yeah, I tried the cheese puffs. Weak. Do you have any tables with actual customers?" I asked.

"Well, sort of. I'll show you." We made our way through the NYU degenerates until we reached our designated "VIP" room, (VIP compared to Hooters.) We called it the "Blue Room" because it was painted royal blue. A few splashes of orange and it could have paid homage to the Mets.

We stood among the crowd at the entrance. Empty martini and highball glasses were scattered haphazardly, some on the floor and a few perched on windowsills. People were spilled all over each other on the sofas, as if preparing for an orgy. If I hadn't known the place was a "business" I would have assumed it was my friends from high school throwing a house party.

"As you can see, I haven't tidied up in here," Carol said, waving her arm around. "I'm a waitress, not a goddamn cleaning service."

At that moment a ridiculously tall, gangly girl with blond hair broke a glass and started shrieking with laughter. Neither Carol nor I moved or cared.

"Doesn't this place breed class? I hope she's not associated with your tables," I said.

"To be honest, I have no clue. People keep moving around."

"OK, just tell me what you need me to do," I said.

"See those fucking clowns over there?" Carol pointed to a table of nine spunky dudes all wearing horn-rimmed glasses and I ♥ New York T-shirts. They were clearly on vacation, or so we hoped.

"The ones with empty champagne glasses in front of them?"

"Yeah, I haven't checked on them in a while. They were super needy. Take them over. They've been here for hours just so they can report on America's rapidly declining culture."

"Ugh, I should go over now, get it over with." The first step in doing something, especially job-related, is always the hardest. I was already wondering about the last shipment of caviar, knowing I could hide in the walk-in cooler once this loser party calmed down and stopped high-fiving each other.

"Good luck," Carol muttered.

"Hi boys," I said, surveying each and every one at the table with contempt. "Why aren't you drinking anything?"

"The other waitress wouldn't come over," said a balding man at the head of the table. I could tell he was the ringleader. I named him Baldie.

"Maybe she didn't like any of you. She passed you off to me, so I think that's a clear indication."

The group laughed nervously, thinking I was kidding around – anxious for alcohol.

"It's kind of you to help us," a dude said from across the table. I couldn't tell if he was being sarcastic or earnest. He looked like he'd fled a salon in the middle of a haircut.

"My pleasure," I said, handing Baldie a menu. I gave the table plenty of time to decide while I smoked another cigarette with Carol in the back near the ice machine. I emphasized to Carol the importance of "doing nothing" because it really seemed like Flask was running itself. I do make it a policy to instill my ideas onto others, and I can be rather convincing at times.

When I eventually returned to the table, Baldie continued to be the spokesperson for the group. He had decided on two bottles of our cheapest sparkling apple wine. I knew darn well we were out of it due to the NYU reunion masking as a fundraiser, but led the table to believe otherwise. Returning to the ice machine area, I captured one of the bussers named Jimmy – and I do mean captured – they're generally a sweet, but sneaky breed. Smarter than us waitstaff for sure, especially when it comes to doing nothing. I designated Jimmy's assignment in broken Spanish. "Bring nine glasses and a champagne bucket with ice to the table. And don't forget the napkins," translated into "*Nuevo vasos. Hielo. Servilletas. Pronto.*" Thankfully, I'd taken the time to learn a couple of key phrases in Spanish in order to do less work. At the time, Flask had yet to hire a busboy that spoke English. I didn't care. In fact, I preferred it. Less unnecessary chit chat.

I lurked in the corner of the Blue Room, watching Jimmy set up the table. Supervising, if you will, glancing at my watch. After he awkwardly completed the task, I considered checking if we received another shipment of "vintage" apple cider. I quickly dismissed that idea, as the stairs were steep, and – let's face it – Laurent was too high by the end of the night to order items we actually needed. Instead, I grabbed two bottles of the sparkling pear wine from behind the bar. Heading over to the table, I assumed the slap-happy group would never know the difference.

I presented the first bottle to Baldie, who looked hard at the label.

"This is the apple?" He questioned me arrogantly.

I held my ground.

"Doesn't *poirré* mean pear in French?" he persisted. *Of course, he was French, how silly of me.*

"Yes, it does," I said. "And did you know pear means apple in English?"

He didn't run with the joke, despite the fact I was laughing, so I followed it up with, "Sir, we're out of apple, but the pear is much better. And because I'm so frigging nice, I'm going to give you the pear for the same price. Taste it. If you're not happy with it, we'll try another goddamn fruit." I felt like I was selling them a chair when they were shopping for a table. I reminded myself that I was in charge. It wasn't like they had a choice. I was clearly the boss, and they were at my mercy.

Unfortunately, after my fantastic spiel, I remembered this was the one bottle I could never get open. I explained this to them and took off to get help. I left the other one on the ice that Jimmy had somehow foraged. Between Jimmy slamming the top of the bottle on a table, and me with a steak knife, we managed to pry it open. I returned to the table in mid-speech about how the *poirré* is the only sparkling wine that requires manpower and a knife to unleash its sweet nectar, but quickly shut up when I noticed the field trip had opened the other bottle and poured it all out for each other. I was astonished and pleased. They did my job for me, and they still had to tip me! How satisfying.

"You guys are great!" I declared, filling up the remaining two glasses. "Self-sufficient, I really like that."

They were just so happy to get some service. Anyway, that's a prime example of doing as little as possible on the

job. An attitude like mine can really cut down on unnecessary stress.

CHAPTER 2

Exceptions To The Rules

Since doing nothing is admittedly boring, I have decided certain actions enhance the fine art of the craft. The actions I list here provide strict enjoyment without much effort. I label these few activities "exceptions."

Obviously, the first and biggest exception is having sex. You are definitely doing something if you are taking part in any sexual act. I don't need to detail the enjoyment that can be obtained by having safe sex. If you're not sure what I'm talking about, then you're either too young to be reading this book, or you should be reading a handbook on sex.

These are the only situations where the exception does not apply:

1. You are a prostitute. It *is* possible to do nothing while getting fucked, if you're just lying there while the action is being done to you. However, it is probably not enjoyable. Also, it's technically considered work – which we hate.
2. You despise the person you are sharing the same bed

(towel, kitchen counter, life, etc.) with, for whatever reasons.

3. You are having sex by yourself. This one is tricky because, yes, you are doing something, but no, no one knows about it unless you have an audience. Or you are standing in front of an open window.

The second exception is drinking. Drinking alcohol literally promotes the act of doing nothing. In fact, the more you drink, the less likely you are to do anything. Since drinking impairs your motor skills, it automatically cuts down on the things you're "allowed to do" as well. Fantastic, I say. Being under the influence is a perfect excuse to avoid driving or operating heavy machinery. Incidentally, an extended period of drinking encourages sleep and further relaxation.

The only times you should not partake in this activity:

1. If you are allergic to alcohol, stick to doing nothing. Going to the hospital falls under the category of doing something arduous and unpleasant.

2. If you are pretending a nonalcoholic drink is actually alcohol. *Not* cool. If you're caught, you will be considered an even bigger loser than you were before. Unacceptable.

3. For some bizarre reason you don't like the effects. Watch a movie instead. However, avoid foreign films with subtitles – way too much thinking.

4. You are teaching a kindergarten class how to paint. You don't want to look like a fool in front of thirty kids that will describe your actions in vivid detail to their parents over dinner.

Drinking alcohol, whether it's white wine spritzers at a luncheon or shots of Jägermeister at a college pub, is a social activity. One could say it loosens us up and takes away our inhibitions, which is why drinking is considered something to do with a reasonable amount of caution. However, if you are accustomed to drinking wisely, often, and among friends, you should be off to a good start.

My ex-husband wore a Calvin and Hobbes T-shirt that had Calvin saying, "If you're not wasted, the day is." I prefer to quote Frank Sinatra, who once said, "I feel sorry for all the people that aren't alcoholics. The best they're going to feel all day is when they get up in the morning."

The third exception is smoking cigarettes or cigars. Smoking cigarettes is a favorite pastime for those who know the true art of procrastination. I'm aware that smoking is a controversial subject and can result in death, so please be clear that I'm not advocating the use of tobacco for anyone who does not already consider him or herself addicted to nicotine.

To those who smoke, however, continue to enjoy it with caution. In addition to providing stress relief, it also prolongs any type of real work. Limiting yourself to half a pack a day is an excellent idea! According to my rough calculations, that should cut your risk of developing lung cancer exactly in half. Those are good odds. I can't imagine dying is enjoyable.

Times when smoking is not advisable:

1. Smoking while filling your gas tank. If you're anywhere near as clumsy as I am, you will go up in flames.

2. Smoking in any restaurant. They recently hung a non-celebrity for lighting up at Spago. (Just joking.)
3. Smoking while teaching a kindergarten class how to paint. First of all, it's bad to smoke in front of kids. Secondly, they will tell on you. (See drinking alcohol above.)

The fourth exception to the rules is eating. Eating fantastic food is not work. Not in my book. Especially in America. Eating is a mindless ritual with which we consume our time for the sake of enjoyment and survival. Not to mention, if we don't eat, twenty-four thousand restaurants will go out of business in the borough of Manhattan alone. I would hate to be held partially responsible for that. I can't imagine all those cute chefs working in retail, using their paring knives to pry open boxes of socks.

Moreover, eating is one of our nation's top sources of entertainment. You might say that dining out is the public's greatest talent. We drink at restaurants, which as you remember, enhances doing nothing. We use restaurants for romantic evenings as a prelude to sex, which is the first, and most important exception to the rules. And, if we are not in California, we can smoke outside of most restaurants. Eating, therefore, becomes a very important exception to the rules.

The only stipulations being these:

1. You're eating at a crab house. Unless it is rather ritzy crab house – and there aren't many – you will be cracking your own shellfish. That's a lot of work. Sometimes, and I know this for fact, the staff will say

they've run out of crackers, just so they can laugh at you. I know this because I've done it. The customer either sits there stupefied or attempts to crack a king crab with his or her silverware. I've seen impatient customers use their car keys when they think no one is looking. It's not a pretty sight. The bottom line is rogue crab houses require too much effort. If you do happen to find yourself in Maryland or Florida, stick to the shrimp cocktail and order a third Bloody Mary. That's my advice.

2. Buffets. Let's not even bring the COVID-19 virus into this. Buffets were a terrible idea long before this global pandemic. Think Atlantic City. Imagine Sizzler if it's still in business. Buffets are exhausting, almost mini projects that you don't get paid for participating in. The better buffets in Las Vegas can actually be quite expensive and have lines longer than Frontier Airlines or Disney World in its heyday. Then you have to wait forever to pile up your plate. Forget the fact that strangers are breathing on your food and breathing on you.

I haven't been anywhere near a buffet in, like . . . thirty years, but in my youth, I found myself standing around assessing them with my family. Judging them as if the Minty family had been hired for quality control. We used to examine the condition of the lettuce and the freshness of the fish, making sure it fit our standards. What a joke. If Wendy's buffet was acceptable, and Pizza Hut's was top of the line, why we debated over Ponderosa Steakhouse, I will never understand.

If, and that's a very big if, you've decided a buffet meets

your criteria, one has to find the right plate and decipher which salad dressing is which. The choices generally lead to complete bewilderment. Then you have to try and keep everything separate on one plate. Gravy gets in your coleslaw . . . beet juice leaks into your cottage cheese . . . it's just gross.

The bottom line is just say "no" to buffets. If others with whom you are *dining* opt for the buffet, you'll look sleek and classy by ordering à la carte off the menu. The women will secretly admire your self-control even though they'll try to talk you out of it. On a similar note, the men will look at you as a dainty creature and perhaps see you in a different light. Except for your own significant other who knows you just HATE buffets.

There is one more activity I must address: sleeping.

Since sleeping is the epitome of doing nothing, this is a gray area and hard to label. All I know is a good night's sleep helps us muster up the energy up for the other four exceptions.

To ensure proper sleep, I suggest a few little tricks prior to bedtime:

1. Extremely satisfying sex with the person of your choice. If you're not in a relationship or don't have a preference, anyone cute and alive will do.
2. Full supplies of Valium, painkillers, or Tylenol PM on hand at all times.
3. If you're one of those anti-drug people, have herbal drugs available such as kava kava, valerian, or melatonin. Just don't come running to me when they don't work.

4. A bed is helpful, although not essential. Sleep shouldn't be a struggle with a hard surface unless you're in a straitjacket. In that case, you would already be pumped up with Valium, so sleeping might not be too difficult. Still, sleeping on the floor just sucks.

Always eat chocolate before bed. It leads to vivid dreams of success. One night after eating chocolate, I dreamed I was best friends with Milton Hershey, and he and I wrote the children's book, *Charlie and the Chocolate Factory* together. Roald Dahl was not in the picture. Milton and I, and a staff of twenty, hired Gene Hackman to star as Mr. Wonka in the film version. I think I'm getting my point across. I love chocolate, and what better time to eat it than midnight?

CHAPTER 3

Where We Stand When It Comes To Decision Making

In everyone's life, there are decisions to be made on a daily basis. Decisions affect actions, which in turn, affect "doing nothing." Some choices are small and probably quite insignificant, yet they still require effort. Milk Duds or Twizzlers at the movies? Shall I dye my hair purple just to be different? Do I say yes when my boyfriend proposes, or do I solicit other offers? Every day, we decide what will happen with some aspect of our lives. I would hate to think we are truly responsible for every mistake. While we love to blame a higher power, I do believe some decisions depend on free will. This is why we should make the fewest number of decisions possible.

First, the minor choices, such as Milk Duds versus Twizzlers at the movies, shouldn't be a struggle. (You should only be spending twenty-three dollars on candy if you're buying five packages, not one, but that's beside the point.) If you really want the candy, you must get it. But decide what you want before you approach the intimidating concession stand. People will always be waiting behind you. It can be eleven thirty in the morning in the most remote suburb – in Montana – and there will still be someone right up your ass. It's just the way life works. If you hesitate or waiver, you'll look moronic. Especially since the candy selection at most movie theaters never varies. To actually not know what you want when it's your turn could indicate a personal growth problem.

Just do what I do. Get both. Then there is no decision to be made.

Now for the semi-important decisions. Do I turn my hair from brown to violet? My answer is, can someone do it for me? I don't want to be doing something extra, and technically unnecessary, by myself.

Then get practical: will it be a hassle to keep up? Will rainy days pose a challenge? Will you be kicked out of your fancy country club? Will it affect your employment? If so, can you afford to quit your job? Are you in any upcoming weddings? Weigh the pros and cons before you enter the salon.

Then again, if you really think it will be fun, then just do it! Deal with the consequences later. You can always wear a baseball cap for the rest of the year. Semi-important decisions only warrant a little more thought than the candy-at-the-movies decision.

What about choices you have to live with for a very long time, even if they are somewhat unimportant in the grand scheme of things? Should I get a tattoo? *Of course, you should.* As a rule, you wouldn't play around with the idea unless you secretly desired it, so just *go for it!* But be smart about it. Opt for a small tattoo in a discreet place rather than a dragon across your forehead. A tattoo decision is really on the same scale as a semi-important decision. Loosen up a bit, and you should have no problem deciding.

Most importantly, personal decisions should never be swayed by what another person thinks. (That doesn't include doctors, psychics, or financial advisors.) Your parents, husband, wife, boyfriend, girlfriend, dog . . . are not you, and neither is your rabbi or priest. The saying rings true: If your mentor jumped off a bridge, would you jump after him?

That leaves us with tough decisions. The life-changing options that will alter your existence. Should I move to Idaho and join that cult that looks so fun? Quit paying taxes and live in a teepee? If you really want to take on the government and live off the land, be my guest. But generally, if that is your mission, you shouldn't have to think it over. You're either a risk-taker, or you're not.

Just an aside, the only reason I'm not ruling Idaho out as a bad idea is that it really seems they don't do much up there except complain. I'd imagine it might be quite a relaxing environment.

Should I adopt a child? Some choices, and you'll know them when they arise, take more consideration than others. A tough decision, yes, but truthfully speaking, you don't have to decide until you see if you're eligible or not. It's more difficult for a hard-working couple in this day and age to adopt a child than it is for a high school senior to be accepted into Harvard. (Angelina Jolie is not a good example, by the way. If I didn't worship the ground she walks on, I would say celebrities have an advantage.)

If you do become eligible to adopt, you should be so honored that the choice is easy. Do it now because you won't want to risk trying again later. The requirements will only get more stringent. Plus, adopting a child is a beautiful thing to do. You can give your love to some little person who is badly in need of it without the pregnancy hassle. For all those who need clarification, having a baby is definitely doing something! There is no getting around that!

Should I get married? See, unfortunately, that takes thought. Any topic that later in life that makes you say "what if?" is tricky. Feeling in charge of your destiny scares some people. (I won't mention any names.) It would be easier to simply float through life assuming everything was predetermined. Unfortunately, that's not practical. Sometimes one can get philosophical, wondering if a higher power is deciding for you and just letting you think you have a choice. Generally, the more you think, the more confused you'll be. Best to simplify the questions that circulate in your mind.

Consider the facts from your individual perspective. On the subject of marriage, for example. Since I'm a woman and, unfortunately, I prefer men, I would ask myself: Do I have a boyfriend? Does he worship me? Do I love him? Can I see myself sitting on a park bench with him when we're both sixty? Do I look angry on that bench? Am I yelling at him?

One important question to always ask yourself is "Will I be happy?" That should help you decide right there. "Will he or she let me do nothing?" should, however, be the deciding factor.

What about taking a stand? Unless you're an activist for a living, it's truly pointless to care. If you just speak your mind and do what you please all day long that means you take a stand without even thinking about it.

What about important issues you should support, even though you really don't care about the outcome? And what if the choices are two bad prospects? (Like most presidential elections.)

And then there are the topics where people simply disagree. Should you hate all hunters because they kill animals for sport? I personally think hunters should go to a shooting range or take up archery instead, but who cares what I think, right? Perhaps they could learn to like golf. Golf focuses on aim quite a bit. (See Chapter 9 for more on golf.)

But here is the catch: I may be against hunting, but I still wear leather pants. So, basically, caring to some extent can be the same as not caring at all. Either one is fine, I think. It takes the pressure off.

Then there is the issue of preference: Do I go to McDonald's or do I go across the street to Burger King? Who do I give my hard-robbed six dollars to for a burger, when they taste pathetically the same? If you don't care, just go to the establishment you can park at more easily. If you prefer the chicken sandwich from McDonald's, but you like the shake better at Burger King, then compromise. Drink Coke with your chicken sandwich from McDonald's.

I personally prefer McDonald's because I can appreciate a copycat. They stole Burger King's concept and got away with it. Although, that is actually a topic of controversy. In all fairness, both McDonald's and Burger King copied White Castle, so kudos to both of them. It's easier to copy a brand than to formulate it, and they realized this well before Shake Shack and Five Guys.

To reinforce and reiterate, the important thing is not to care. If a tricky situation arises, don't do a thing.

I will now elaborate on an earlier example from my personal life:

Sidebar: This situation took place at the same job/ hellhole I spoke about in Chapter One. On my way to Flask, I used to buy caffeine-free Coke. I chose the caffeine-free option because I love soda, but caffeine sometimes makes me feel like doing something; hence I avoid caffeine at all costs.

One afternoon I was strolling to work and I stopped at my regular deli on Fifth Avenue. I walked straight to the coolers in the back, trying not to dillydally near the chips, and noticed there was only one can of caffeine-free Coke left. I needed three to get through the night. (I only drink soda out of cans. Plastic bottles simply don't get as cold.) Supposedly, drinking out of cans causes cancer in laboratory animals, but I was not and never would be a laboratory animal. I was also a smoker. I figured the cigarettes would shorten my life before drinking out of a can would take its evil effects.

I glanced around, unsure of what to do, my eyes darting from the chips and back to the cooler. I spotted numerous cans of caffeine-free Pepsi nearby. A whole rack of them. Pepsi either had better distribution, or it wasn't as popular as Coke. It had never occurred to me to buy caffeine-free Pepsi, but it should have.

Then I had a great idea. *I should do a taste test! That wastes time at work! How fun!* I bought one can of each and two packages of Doritos. It was early Saturday evening and entering Flask was like walking through an empty, dark graveyard. Plenty of time for experiments.

Laurent was checking out his appearance in the coat check mirror when I walked in. He always looked the same. French, in a cute, American way, unless he was screaming and yelling, then he wasn't quite so adorable.

"Hello, Aimmeé." We kissed each other on both cheeks.

"Laurent," I said, pointing inside my deli bag. "I'm going to do a taste test. Would you like to participate?"

"Oh, Aimmeé, that's why we love you," he mumbled more to himself than to me. "Carol's upstairs."

I quickly changed my shoes and scampered upstairs with the soda, looking for Carol. I knew she'd have an opinion. I found her in the back, sitting on an upside-down bucket, smoking a cigarette and reading *Boy's Life* magazine. She must have been bored.

"Yo, whaaaaaaat's upppppppp?" I shouted, announcing my presence. (Just for the record, I was doing this long before Michael Scott in *The Office*.) Her hands went straight to her face as if to shield herself from an impending attack. Once she saw it was me, she acted all super cool again.

"Oh, you know, blah, blah, blah. Your hair looks great, what did you do?" she asked me.

"Woke up from my nap and slicked it with gel," I said. "Look, we're going to do a taste test," I continued, pulling out my cans of soda. I opened them both and set them in a champagne bucket filled with ice, meant for the stupid customers. I reached for some clean glasses and proceeded to pour shots of caffeine-free Coke and Pepsi.

"Oh, how cute. You've never done this before?" she

remarked.

"You have?" She was full of surprises.

"Yeah, I was in, like, third grade."

"Carol, I'm sure you didn't do it with caffeine-free versions," I said, rolling my eyes. "We didn't even know what caffeine meant back then. It's not like we were sipping lattes before we hopped on the yellow school bus."

"You're probably right," she said, tossing the magazine on the floor.

"Close your eyes while I mix these up so you're confused," I instructed, juggling the glasses. I had to concentrate so *I* didn't mix them up. "OK! Open your eyes." I handed her the glass with caffeine-free Coke in it.

She took a sip. "Alright. Let me cleanse my palate with one of your Doritos."

"Absolutely not. That might affect your taste buds," I said, handing her the Pepsi.

"I like the second one better," she said. "I prefer Pepsi, that's why."

"Wow." I was beyond impressed. "You could actually taste the difference?"

"Well, not really, but Coke has more carbonation. I'm not into super-fizzy drinks."

"Could have fooled me," I laughed. "Weren't we the ones guzzling champagne straight out of the bottle last night? Standing in this same exact spot."

"That doesn't count."

"This is actually interesting. I bet most people aren't aware of the carbonation factor. I bet Laurent doesn't know that."

"Amy, French people don't drink gallons of soda like we Americans do."

"Sure they do. They just mix it with gin."

At that point, I had Carol give me the test, but I cheated. Out of the corner of my eye, I watched her pour the Coke.

The Pepsi was definitely better, I thought. Twenty-seven years of drinking Coke instead of Pepsi. What a fool I'd been. But the best part of being ignorant is that you don't know how stupid you are. I handled the truth OK, though. I did. I told myself everything was going to be just fine. I knew I'd still buy Coke if there wasn't Pepsi available. I wasn't going to stress out if it was Coke they served in a restaurant or anything.

You must remember that the little things are not so important. Remember that learning is voluntary. So is listening. The Coke/Pepsi taste test is a roundabout example of a little decision. A small choice to make in life. As I was mulling all this over, I was staring at a large pipe dripping water onto the floor. I didn't bother to tell anyone. I just enjoyed the fact that it wasn't my problem. I knew that *little drip* would result in a rainfall in the downstairs bar, so I rejoiced in the fact that I wasn't working downstairs that night. Fewer puddles to hop over.

At that moment Laurent busted through the door interrupting our privacy.

"Girls, it's raining downstairs. Where is the bucket?" he asked.

"I don't know. Do the taste test, Laurent," Carol said, not wanting to give up her seat. She shoved two glasses in his direction.

"What is this? Coke verses Pepsi? You stupid Americans," he said, grinning until he observed the cans nestled on ice. He made a face. "We are low on ice, girls."

"It's caffeine-free," I chirped.

"I hate caffeine-free drinks," he said, swigging the rest of my glass. "Yeah, it's terrible." He cringed and handed me the empty glass. "Where is the papo?" he asked, referring to the busser.

"Check the kitchen," I said, "He was cooking eggs with the dishwasher before."

The point of my story, for those who are confused, is that it's OK to have preferences as long as you don't go out of your way to make sure you get it. If both options are available, pick the one you prefer. If they're not, choose something else. Do not walk all over a town looking for Bonkers candies when you suspect those delightful fruity chews were probably discontinued.

Now, what if you belong to a union, but you don't really care to vote or go to meetings because it seems like a pain in the ass? If you're nodding your head, *yes, this is me,* you're just like all the rest of us. Don't bother going!

If you belong to the Screen Actors Guild, like I did for many years, and don't even understand why they're on strike, then you probably aren't very active in your organization. Not to mention you're not getting much work – through the union – because if you were, you'd find out by accident. Consequently, if they call you to picket, and you don't feel like it, don't do it. Just because the union might have rightly assumed you'd be doing nothing doesn't mean you have to spend your day marching around holding a sign. One more strike won't make a difference. As long as you pay your dues, they can't fire you from their little club. It's a union, remember.

Last, but not least, sometimes we are thrown into actions due to circumstances beyond our control. Weather is a good example. It's a force of nature that probably doesn't even know humans exist. Natural disasters can strike people at unfortunate times, and I don't mean having to buy an umbrella when it rains.

Earthquakes, for example, can cause death and destruction to homes. So can hurricanes and tornadoes, for those of you who never saw *The Wizard of Oz*. Being a victim of a natural disaster affects your life and forces you to do something. You are not presented with a choice. Similarly, fighting a disease is not an option. It's an unfortunate and disturbing aspect of life. This is the only reason why doctors have my blessing when it comes to doing more than I advocate others do.

To sum up: don't sweat decisions. Just be sensible and ask yourself, how much work will my choice entail?

CHAPTER 4

Doing This And Doing That: Why Bother?

Have you ever found yourself in a situation where the people around you are so annoyingly exuberant over the stupidest things? It's like an awakening, when, all of a sudden, you realize you only like about a third of the people you hang out with (if that), and you can't force a smile to save your life.

Sometimes, you might even look to the active leader of your Quasimodo group and consider wringing his or her neck. You wonder why you've allowed yourself to be a pawn in their massive game of chess. Who said they could arrange all these elaborate plans for everyone? Who gave them the right? And the funny thing is, you've never realized your anger over this until this very second. Suddenly, it's clear. Allow me to elaborate . . .

Perhaps it's one of those nights where you would have been much happier hanging out by yourself and ordering a movie, but you promised "so and so" you'd go to the opening of some bullshit impressionist-style art gallery. You felt like laying low, but instead you need to muster up the energy to mingle with tall people wearing heels in order to discuss

Renoir all night.

Ask yourself why.

The clock ticks – now it's quarter to seven. Are you still in your yoga pants, watching HBO instead of ironing your trendiest outfit? Knowing there is a damn good reason you don't even own an iron. Do you loathe yourself for agreeing to those plans and sit there thinking of excuses not to go?

Hello? Is there any reason to do stuff you don't feel like doing? Just because you said you would? Chances are, you were caught off guard when you were invited. It's technically not your fault.

I can recall countless times I came home from an evening out, reeking of booze and stale cigarettes, trying to analyze where I'd just been and why. Finally, the day came when I could admit to myself that it hadn't been much fun. In fact, if I hadn't been so drunk, it would have been so bloody boring I would have fallen asleep ordering another drink.

In my mid-twenties, I spent roughly eight months in Las Vegas gambling and partying every day, and I'm still resenting the fact that I wasted so much precious energy and time. Let's not even talk about the fact I slept two hours a night to go from twenty grand to a couple of twenty-five dollar chips. One day, I woke up and took a car to the airport. Got my ass back to New York, where life made sense. Even then, when I think about it, I wanted the freedom to do nothing.

If you've ever felt like this, here is what you need to do to break the vicious cycle of wasting your time:

First of all, sit down and make a list of the people you would do a week in jail for (real jail, as in federal prison. Not some sweet deal in Malibu.) You will find that your list of friends has been narrowed considerably. Then think of the people, on that list, who would do a week in jail for you. The list may be narrowed down further. Do not include the men or women that would do jail time for you in exchange for a sexy conjugal visit. Be honest with yourself.

OK, so now we have our list of important people. Ask yourself if you have a good time with them without relying massively on at least two exceptions to the rules. Basically, can you carry on a conversation with them without reaching for your cigarettes or trying to get the bartender's attention? If he or she opens their mouth to speak, is the sex ruined? You get the picture.

Post the list on your refrigerator. Do not put a title on the list in case any relatives, friends, or potential partners happen to drop by. Even if they don't act curious, they will be. Knowing you're not invited to a private party is never a good feeling. So don't label your list. Let them wonder, because that's better than the truth. It's actually pretty funny, because they'll be rightfully upset over something they don't understand. However, there's no need to destroy another person's day just to remind yourself who matters.

Next, make another list of the things you've done with people that you never want to do again. For instance: the time over the summer when you suffered through that period piece on the French Revolution at the Independent Film Center that had no air-conditioning. Or the time you slept with your boring neighbor, Fred, just to spice up a pool party. Whatever it may be, write it all down and stick it *inside* your refrigerator to remind yourself of your previous mistakes. The list might be long – you might have to clear a shelf and throw out that box of Entenmann's donuts. Since you likely open the refrigerator at least ten times a day even when you're not hungry it's a good place to keep reminders.

Make sure you identify all ringleaders. Ringleaders are the people that are good at persuading you about how much you'd be missing if you didn't tag along. They can be very clever and manipulative when they start discussing wasted opportunities and ticking clocks. Don't believe them. Remember that your presence makes other people look good! No wonder they're always trying to get you to join them. Save your energy for the stuff *you* want to do.

Ringleaders will also try and get you at the last minute. Beware that you might be a fill-in for someone else who was smart enough to back out in the nick of time. Who wants to be second choice? Please. If they call you half an hour before the play starts, forget it!

This might be the most important thing to take away from this chapter: NEVER ANSWER YOUR PHONE. That's why caller ID and voicemail were invented. Not to mention it could be your boss or prick manager calling on your day off. It's not worth the risk. If they have something important to say, they'll leave a message. (More on this subject in Chapter 16.)

Just remember to do exactly what you feel like doing, providing you are able. If you feel like ripping up the town and chugging champagne through a funnel, then you'll be the one calling up people to join you. If no one feels like going, go out by yourself. It can be really fun, especially with lots of money in a great city. (A little less fun on the outskirts of Detroit without a car, but try and make the most of your situation.) If you have a hangover and would feel better sipping a homemade Piña Colada or a ginger ale while watching the Travel Channel, rather than blowing all your money at the bar with people that bore you, you best find your blender. As long as you can still plug it in successfully, you won't be sorry.

If you're unsure whether you really want to do something, it's better to err on the side of caution. I've been camping in Maine where skunks were known to spray daily. (This was obviously when I was still a kid and things were out of my control.) I've been to Delaware when I knew a hurricane was approaching. (Same situation. Thanks Mom.) I've put money into investments I was uneasy about. (That was my fault.) I've picked jobs that I knew reeked of danger. (At least they were fun!) I've dated people that bounced in and out of jail. (Also fun!) But today, I look back and think, "Why?"

No one is perfect. Striving for excellence is a ridiculously impossible concept. Strive to do fewer things you're not jazzed about. Hopefully, you can look upon your life in the same way. You rule *it*. Don't let *it* rule *you*.

CHAPTER 5

Optimal Career Choices That Emphasize Doing Nothing

My adventures thus far have taught me an important lesson. Ironically, a life of doing nothing can be sustained, in the long-term, by having an education. Who knew? I would like to make life easier for kids by reaching them in their high school years, when they can still plan their better-paying futures doing as little as possible in a systematic manner. I take that back. Don't wait until high school. You should have thought about that around age ten. That's the appropriate age these days. Used to be sixteen or seventeen. Or twenty-five, if you grew up privileged. The younger you are, the more choices you have. Later in life, the options you're stuck with don't pay as well.

The most effective plan is to select an education or experiences that will further your growth in a specific field of nothing. I suggest the following areas of study:

◆ Psychologist

If I didn't have to go back to school to be legally employed as a high-paid counselor, I would opt for this occupation in a heartbeat. When I was growing up, I met my role model at Disneyland: Alan Thicke, the psychiatrist on ABC's *Growing Pains*. It was the highlight of my youth. No one could understand why.

The man was an icon. His character embodied the simplicity of life. He even worked from home! His primary duty was pretending to listen to his clients' woes. He lived in a nice house, had a wonderful, nuclear family, and all he had to do was sit there and listen to people bitch about their lives a few times a day. Sounds amazing to me, and he did it in the eighties and nineties. Just saying.

For the amount of money therapists charge, you could listen to anything. As a psychologist, you simply have to sit there and make your patient feel uncomfortable and weird. All you have to do is hold this inquisitive, yet pensive stare and evaluate your client's actions. Once you've labeled them, you can float back into your own sunny thoughts about where to dine that evening with their money.

You can do nothing – all day – as long as you keep that serious look on your face and half pay attention. In the past, this was the all-time best job in the world, because therapists never said a word. How did they even get away with it? It was the most fabulous con.

Most psychologists I've seen in real life – and there have been a few over the years – rarely speak. Although they've gotten better at commenting because suckers in 2020 are getting pissed off. People want answers these days and no longer accept paying hundreds of dollars an hour for judgmental silence. Not receiving feedback is no longer good enough, and therapists have finally come to realize this. But still, all you need is some catch phrases at the ready. Statements that make you appear understanding. "That is totally unfair!" works in any situation. If you remember this, you're golden. Most shrinks will even tape record patients so they don't have to remember anything the patient says. Rewind the tape and answer any perplexing questions in the client's next session.

All you have to do is "evaluate your patient" while sneaking glances at the ticking clock, and end each session with, "Over the next few days try to examine *why* you feel that way. Then we'll gather our thoughts the following week." This is the part where you guide your patient toward the exit. This will also be the only time you have to rise from the chair in the forty-five minute time slot. Rising to the occasion, so to speak. *Goodbye and good luck. Get the fuck out of my office!*

Did you ever wonder why psychologists go straight to your file when you walk in the room? Or have it available on their small table next to their big coffee mug filled with gin? It's because they can't remember your name. They might retain how they spent your money, but your name? That remains a puzzle until the file is reopened. This means you don't even need a good memory to work in this field. There are so many positives to this job, I feel overcome with regret that I did not consider it as a future goal at age ten.

Some people think psychologists take their patients' problems home with them. I sincerely doubt that. That would be like someone who works in a supermarket pricing the food for fun in his or her own kitchen. Very unlikely. Plus, if you're a non-listening psychologist in the first place, it's doubtful your client's problems would haunt you once you returned home. Those who can afford a psychologist essentially can't be that bad off, so if you choose this profession, never feel like you're taking advantage of people. Most of the world can't afford you.

Sidebar: I swore off any type of therapy years ago because I found I was always jealous of the therapist's easy life. So, apparently, counseling is not a concept that's fizzling out quite yet. What's it all about? I think therapists must acquire a third of their clients based on the certitude that some people absolutely love to hear the sound of their own voice echoing through a quiet room.

♦ Nutritionist

Sorry, but what's so hard about advising people to go on a low-fat, high-fiber diet? At least that was the old rule. In 2020, add fifty more grams of protein while removing all sugar from your diet, and you've given some solid, noteworthy advice. I was in my car the other day when the radio denounced the "food pyramid." A tool I was forced to memorize and practice while growing up was suddenly a load of shit and ridiculed for promoting obesity. I was laughing so hard, I parked like a jackass and almost hit a woman's cart as she stormed out of Marshall's.

Bottom line: Being a nutritionist is a dream job. The same rules apply to everyone, with the exception of those with specific food allergies or chronic conditions. Then all you have to say is, "I understand you have a bad reaction to tomatoes. Stop eating them." The extra step is annoying – no question – but not the end of the world.

Here's the deal: Martha has hypertension, and she's reaching forty. Tom is sixty-six, and is at high risk for prostate cancer. Lily is two hundred pounds and suffering from an underactive thyroid. Noreen is certain she's afflicted with fibromyalgia because she self-diagnoses herself all day long with tests she downloads off the internet. George is seventy-five and routinely tested for rheumatoid arthritis since it runs in his family.

Guess the fuck what? They should all be on a low-fat, high-fiber, high-protein diet. That's right: oatmeal for breakfast, seared tuna over greens for lunch, and a dinner consisting of boneless chicken breast and steamed spinach. No table salt allowed! Could this job be any easier? Nutritionists just tell you what nonsense to eat and how much of it to consume in one sitting. (Six ounces of tuna, whatever.) I feel like I could do that simply by looking at the person and prescribing the opposite of my eating habits.

It's not like you have to follow the advice you're dishing out – no pun intended. There's no way I would. In my opinion, chefs are in charge of cooking and creating fantastic food. Eat their food, just less of it. (It will taste better, believe me.)

Nutritionists don't perform any magic tricks; they give advice. It's entirely up to their clients to alter bad habits and pick up a tennis racket every once in a while.

Even if you knew absolutely nothing about nutrition, all you'd have to do is open up any copy of *Shape* or *Fitness* magazine. I have this month's issue of *Fitness* right here. Unread up until now, but if I turn to page five, the writer tells us to substitute one cup of grapes for a half-cup of raisins. I'm not even sure she's right. It's more like two tablespoons, and I have zero knowledge on the subject. According to the same writer, instead of a 1.5-ounce bag of banana chips (which is always my snack of choice – NOT) we should eat a regulation banana. I'd continue down the list here, but I think I've proven my point. Anyone with a third of a brain could be a nutritionist.

I think the best would be to work at WW (formally Weight Watchers) or Jenny Craig and prescribe literally the same diet for everyone. How funny would that be? In places like that, people join strictly to lose weight. Rarely do employees have to worry about much else. Although, having said that, I bet weighing people in once a week might be a challenge. I'm sure for as many people that lose weight on the program, more people gain it. I, for one, love some of WW's snacks. The ice cream sandwiches sold in supermarkets remind me of grammar school. However, when I purchase a box of six, I'll eat them all in one sitting. I'm no expert, but I'm pretty sure that's not the way to lose weight.

Sidebar: The thought of being a bored nutritionist was so tempting to me at one time that I actually considered going back to school for it. I got so inspired that I decided to spend some money toward a class at NYU. I figured I'd start with Basic Nutrition. What a lot of work that turned out to be!

We had to complete a major assessment project on ourselves. It was not the most inspiring assignment. It entailed keeping a food diary on everything we ate for seven days, then applying the nutritional guidelines to it. (I had to read an issue of Shape every morning to refresh my memory on basic nutrition; it had been so long since I'd considered eating healthy.) So the calories, nutrients, and vitamins I inhaled were all added together to compound a disheartening figure. I won't even go into the details.

A few months later, after the class was long over and well out of my mind, my mother was visiting me in Manhattan and found my finalized report thrown haphazardly on my kitchen floor. She picked it up and started reading my food diary like a nosy parent. I didn't think I had much to hide, but reconsidered when I saw her clutching her stomach with laughter.

"You were honest! What are you, crazy?" she howled, from her hunched over position on the floor. Once I saw what she was reading, I knew I should have discarded it properly.

"Honest about what?" I asked, innocently.

"This . . . this!" She smacked the cover sheet of my report. I had titled it "Eating on the Edge," even though it hadn't required an official title.

"It's easier if you're candid on these types of projects," I said. "Less thinking involved."

My mother pointed to a paragraph on page three. "One day you ate six fat-free brownies and thirty slices of 2% Kraft American cheese singles, and you admitted to it!" she howled.

"Well, in my defense, it was more to do with packaging. They sell six brownies to a box and thirty Kraft singles at a time. It makes perfect sense to me to spread it out over one day," I said, refusing to be criticized for my solid good sense. Based on my diet, I'd be dead anyway before I had to succumb to my mother's unsolicited opinions.

Sarah Minty flipped through the remainder of "Eating on the Edge" while I continued to defend myself. "Hey, I went to Go Sushi at least twice that week. That equals two seaweed salads. I try to eat something green at least twice a week."

She gave me a look and flipped to the last page. "You still eat Twinkies?" she asked.

"That's all I ate that day. It was a box of ten. The Sno-Caps and popcorn were consumed after midnight. They count toward the following day."

Sarah Minty simply raised her eyebrows.

"OK, so I'm not nutritionist material. You've proven your point."

"Can I keep this?" my mother asked.

"You're the one who found it. Finders keepers."

"It's cute how you still say that."

I shrugged. "The last jewelry store didn't think so."

My mother tucked "Eating on the Edge" into her bag. "I'm saving this for when I need a good laugh."

"Understandable. You do live in Philly."

Many months later, my dear sweet mother called me up after reading the final analysis. She'd had too much wine and was choking and crying with laughter. According to my calculations, I ate well over 4,000 calories a day and my sodium limit exceeded ten times the recommended amount. My carbohydrate-to-protein ratio was twelve-to-one, and my fat-to- protein ratio was an unsettling ten-to-one. Oh well. According to my detailed charts, I was at risk for heart disease, diabetes, high blood pressure, insanely high cholesterol, aneurysms (whatever those are), liver and kidney disease, anemia, and involuntary seizures. Seizures?

According to those stupid charts, I should have been gaining two pounds a week on average, enjoying shortness of breath and collapsing on the floor from time to time. And yet, I felt healthy as a horse. Furthermore, how could I have been at risk for anemia with all the calories I was consuming? It just didn't make any sense to me.

Anyway, that was the only nutrition course I took at NYU. (It also required a nifty two-hour lab once a week, but that will be discussed in Chapter 7.) After paying the hefty bill, I realized it would be cheaper to goof off at Brooklyn Tech.

Conclusion: Decide on your nothing career before you go to college the first time!

♦ Movie Critic

It pains me to report that one has to possess a journalistic background to qualify for this job. You would think that the people with the most time on their hands would be perfect for this occupation. People like me. Imagine getting paid to comment on movies? That would be like winning the lottery along with a free supply of soda and popcorn. Oh well . . .

♦ Inventor

How many nights do I lie awake in bed trying to come up with an idea so clever that I'll never have to work again? About six out of seven. The best idea I've come up with so far is an indoor roller skating rink for the home, but I'm going to keep thinking. All you need is the idea, and the marketing all comes later by some rich, foolhardy company that believes in your product. Future morons.

Sometimes you can sell your idea and that way you don't have to worry if it ever takes off. I mean, who knew veggie burgers would fly off the shelves? Your best bet is to copy someone else's successful invention and upgrade it. Apply the same principal I used to write research papers in college. If you reword the sentence, it's not really copying.

A college education in science would marginally increase your chances in regards to being an inventor. Mainly, because you'd be in the right environment, among other thinkers that you could listen to and copy from. And you might come across some rare formula to treat those with chronic nosebleeds by just being in a lab. Remember, man invented bread by knocking their beer into a bowl of flour.

Final conclusion: Rule out any other jobs I haven't listed!

CHAPTER 6

Job Choices If The Future Is Now

I realize that many of you might be reading this book later in life, after your college years are over (or never took place). If so, you're essentially in the same boat as I am, trying to find the easiest, highest-paying job in the world. Since the highest-paying jobs usually require the most qualifications, we should aim instead to find the easiest work.

Concentrate on jobs that have the most perks. For example, if everyone you care about still lives in Russia, and you live in the United States, then go work for an airline or a telephone company. You'll enjoy free airfare and long-distance calls. Or perhaps you have a thing for cosmetics. Upscale department stores, for instance, provide you with hands-on access to quality makeup and hygiene products. Once you learn how to switch off those cameras, you should be able to swipe an unlimited supply of Lancôme essentials any day of the week.

Make sure, however, that the perks match your lifestyle. If you're not big on skin care, moisturizers and cleansing products don't have a very high resale value. If you don't drink, why would you work in a liquor store? If you become a professional fisherman, I would encourage you to like fish for dinner. (Lobster, in fact!)

Personally speaking, I've always chosen restaurants and bars to work in simply to maximize on the exceptions to the rules, free of cost. My father once called it "subsidizing." I call it "capitalizing." I feel like my employer is my sponsor; what they don't supply me in earnings, I make up for in food and drink.

In addition to desperate attempts at procuring perks from any dead-end job, doing nothing should remain top priority. Ultimately, does the job allow you to stand around and get paid?

Years ago there were jobs that didn't require much, if any, education. I bring you back to a more carefree time, unlike today's world:

♦ Working in a Video Store

There were few things more satisfying than walking into Blockbuster on a Sunday afternoon, with the whole day ahead of you to watch movies. I can only imagine that working there would have been similar. After all, there was always a television balanced precariously, displaying the employee's favorites. I would have been quite happy to phase out and watch reruns of *Meatballs* and *Pretty in Pink* all day long. Apart from fiddling with the ancient computer and extensive reaching, the workday would have been relatively easy. Video stores were peaceful environments as long as the shop didn't have *Friday the 13th* marathons blaring from every television monitor. I've listed some additional advantages.

• The hours were flexible and attractive. No one woke up to rent a movie at six thirty in the morning. (Except maybe me, who never went to bed.)

• Your customers were usually in a good mood because they had time to rent a movie.

Anyone irate, due to the lack of new releases available, could easily be persuaded to take their business elsewhere.

• You had free access to movies. (If you didn't, I'm positive you could "borrow" a different movie each night and never bring it back.) Just think of the movie knowledge you'd gain from working at a video store. You'd also be the first one to get your hands on the best new thrillers.

The whole trick to working in a video store was figuring out how to open your own video enterprise. It may have been satisfying to make a good, solid living renting out used copies of B-movies, the majority of them starring Eric Roberts.

♦ Working as a Photo Developer:

If you were fired from Blockbuster – trust me, it's possible – you could work in a photo lab. Actually in today's world, this type of job is still an option. It's like viewing the rest of the world through others' lenses. Your friend's and relative's golden moments always look so tame and boring when they show you their pictures. That's because they're not showing you the good ones! The employees at the photo lab are privy to the steamy versions of Sal and Linda's trip to Mt. Everest. Sal and Linda only show you the stupid mountain.

Just in case you're not aware of it, people continue to take some wild photos like they're still living in the 70s and throwing key parties on the weekends. Wild partners love to drop off reels of naked, interactive photos, not once pausing to consider that the quiet, introverted developer is busy making copies for his or her own collection. If you were to wander into the employee's home, you'd probably find a poster-size version of your naked butt processing in his dark bathroom.

Working in a photo lab can also provide you with a "free" camera and plenty of "free" film. If, however, you're not a voyeur and documenting strangers' precious moments doesn't rate high on your list of a good time, then don't bother filling out the application. Working at a religious bookstore might be more your speed.

♦ Planning the Seating Arrangements in an Empty
    Restaurant (Hostess):

This job is so easy, it's incredible. Boring, yes, but boring is better than hard. You can stand around smoking a cigarette or wiping down a menu or two while you contemplate inventions that will make you rich.

However, the restaurant must be doing badly, otherwise management will be up your ass to appear busy. It doesn't matter to you if they're not doing any business because, don't forget, you're only being paid by the hour. You're golden until they have to remove your job from the payroll, which indicates the place is going to shut down shortly anyway. In that case, don't worry, there are still plenty of really awful restaurants out there.

♦ Participating in Surveys and Experiments for the "Good" of Medical Research:

Some of you may never have pictured this as falling under the headline of a job, but let me tell you, it's like striking it rich for a couple hours. All you have to do is sit there and answer their personal questions honestly. You could lie, but I don't suggest screwing up medical research for the next generation.

The work is sometimes difficult to find, but it is available. Hit up medical schools that are located near you. They pay between fifteen and fifty dollars an hour to pick your limited brain. Take your time answering each question and provide a thorough answer. Extrapolate if that's what it takes to lengthen your time sheet. Each extra minute puts more money in your pocket.

Now, if you're on the daring side, you can also sign up to be their guinea pig when it comes to drug testing. You get free drugs, and you get paid. The reason it pays well is because they're never really sure what the side effects might be, so make sure to get some second opinions before you sign on. If you participate in any programs like this *you* are the research – literally. You can look back on it and feel good, knowing you helped create a statistic.

Once, I participated in a clinical trial for a rather notorious pharmaceutical company. Like a little hamster, I went on a seizure-controlling sedative for twenty-eight days. (This was after I learned I was at risk for seizures, according to my nutrition report.) Since I had never experienced anything even resembling a seizure, the drug just made me drowsy and numb. Sometimes people would tap me on the shoulder and I wouldn't feel it. It actually encouraged me to do nothing, if you can believe that. As if I needed encouragement.

Being an utter zombie for a month paid my bills and bought me a nice gold watch, back when gold was affordable. It was definitely worth it. Plus, with a nothing job it doesn't really matter if you're medicated. If you're a good planner, it means you can get the money from two nothing jobs at the same time.

Women out there: Beware of medical research teams offering you up to twenty thousand dollars to donate an egg. You are not a hen. If it sounds too good to be true, I've usually tried it, and it's either dangerous or a scam. Even though I have avoided the "egg trap" thus far, I'm willing to bet whatever technique they use to extract these eggs messes up something else in your body. You'd hardly miss the eggs I'm sure, but the repercussions could be devastating. After all, the companies are offering compensation before the procedure even gets underway!

I bet if they only offered a hundred dollars, they'd get more donations. I think they've underestimated the skepticism of the American population.

♦ Working as an Extra on a Movie Set:

This only applies to people who, by some stroke of luck or cold, calculated move, have landed themselves in the Screen Actors Guild. If you're not eligible to join, skip to the next job.

Blending into the scenery for the sake of art is the epitome of doing nothing. You are not acting. You are barely noticed and sometimes they don't even use you, especially on those high-budget films where production has no idea who's really there. It's usually a long day of doing nothing, eating for free, and catching up on your reading. Occasionally, throughout the day, you might have to take some directorial advice on which way you should stand, but that's about it.

Most extra work takes place in bars, restaurants, parks and similar environments. If you get lucky, you might get to sit there, eating and smoking through the actual shooting.

The only time I ever got royally screwed was when they had me on a set in New Jersey for the short-lived TV show *Ed*. At seven a.m., on a rainy day, the director assigned me as the designated jogger in the background. Why did he pick *me* out of fifty people? Maybe the bastard thought I could use the exercise. I learned never to wear sneakers again on a random shoot. It obviously gave the wrong impression.

After twenty takes of the same shot in the pouring rain, I was about to kill someone. I was so tired that some extras were walking faster than my jogging. On the twenty-first take, I ran into the nearby Dunkin' Donuts and didn't come out. I was then reprimanded and threatened by one of the assistant directors. I apologized profusely, claiming I was hypoglycemic and badly in need of a donut.

Unfortunately, he let me back in the scene, but at least he let me sit on the bench. I vowed never to do that show again. That was, however, the only unfortunate experience I've had being an extra. The rest of the time has been great. One day, on the set of *Vanilla Sky*, the director didn't use me for fifteen hours, and then he let me go home. (It was the same day David Blaine was freezing himself in a block of ice in Times Square.) I got paid $250 for that day of doing nothing besides fretting over David Blaine's chances of survival.

If you don't have an education, and consequently think you don't have much of a future, some places of employment offer excellent opportunities for scams and outright stealing. Just be prepared to flee the country shortly after. These are some I suggest:

♦ Working in a Bank:

I know it's obvious, but it really is the best place to pack a bag of money and race to the border in an unmarked car. If you actually work there, it eliminates the need for a gun. If you've been a longtime employee, you may even be *trusted*.

♦ Working for a Mass-Producing Jewelry Factory:
(I don't endorse any type of theft from the mom and pop shops.)

My mother had a friend who worked at Cartier for THIRTY YEARS! Talk about missed opportunities. Her twenty-ninth year could have been what we call a "golden year." No pun intended. I guess she didn't want to live the remainder of her life on the run, but if you're young, I say go for it! Just think: pawnshops still exist for this very reason.

♦ Working at a Parking Garage or a Valet Service:

On your first and only night on the job, nab the sweetest car, switch the plates, and drive across the border to the first used car dealership. However, if you do attempt this, don't drive over the speed limit. That would be like juggling an antique vase right before you auction it off to the highest bidder.

Keep in mind, these options provide you with the opportunity to make a lot of money in one shot. An enormous amount of cash gives you the freedom to do nothing for a long time. Think about it.

These are some ideas I don't suggest:

♦ Stealing from a Casino:

Bad idea. The mob is very clever. More clever than the police force. They will hunt you down and kill you. If they can't find you they will stalk your remaining family members and use them as colorful bait.

♦ Scamming Nightclubs and Strip Clubs:

Same thing. I repeat: The mob is very clever. If you're a dancer or manager, make money off the chump customers. Do *not* mess around with the owner's profits. He or she will know.

♦ Kidnapping an Important Person for Ransom:

This might seem easy, but I can assure you – it's not. Plus, you can't kidnap someone unless you're prepared to kill them, and I'm not promoting killing of any sort in this book. Not only will you more than likely be caught, you'll be caught committing a federal crime. Federal crime translates into federal prison. They work you to death in there, which makes doing nothing impossible.

CHAPTER 7

The Tragedy Of Mistaking Hobbies For Potential Jobs

Doing nothing is always the most rewarding when you're supposed to be doing something else. That's why doing nothing at work is the ultimate goal. There is, however, certain enjoyment to be gained from doing something pleasurable. Let's call these random quests for inner fulfillment "hobbies." Generally, everyone has one or two hobbies to simply keep entertained.

My more practical definition of a hobby goes something like this: a derivative of having fun, which is often enhanced by the four exceptions to the rules: having sex, drinking, eating, and smoking.

An example of this would be reading, or doing arts and crafts, while drinking wine. (I'm sure some of us are still gluing sticks of wood together for fun.) Regardless, a hobby is an exercise that involves slight concentration and brings you some type of satisfaction. For some, it might be cooking or baking, catching up on current events, or decorating your home.

The important thing to remember is that hobbies need to remain in their own particular category. Attempting to turn a hobby into anything job-related only brings needless pain and suffering. I must stress this fact because one could easily be misled into thinking, "Hey, let's try and get paid for doing something we enjoy!"

Unfortunately, life doesn't work that way.

Take me, for example: My hobbies revolve around the exceptions to the rules. Anything else would be more of a secondary interest. Perhaps reading magazines and maxing out my credit card at the mall would fall under this category. I'd really have to think about what else I honestly like doing.

The fact of the matter is I wouldn't be able to take any one of the exceptions to the rules and turn it into a money-making opportunity. If I had sex all day for money, I don't think I'd take pleasure in it any longer. I'm also quite sure other unanticipated problems would crop up.

Drinking alcohol twenty-four-seven for a decent paycheck? I'd probably like it at first, but after a week or so I might notice that my brain cells were rapidly disappearing, along with my youth. Worse things could happen, of course. In addition, alcohol is a broad category, and if I had to sample scotch and bourbon all day, I wouldn't be happy.

Eating all day would be gross. I wouldn't even consider that. I might have to eat items I hate, too, knowing my luck. Things like tofu and liver. I'd end up binging on the good stuff and becoming a traditional bulimic or hugely obese. (There are very few skinny food critics out there.)

I'm not a doctor, but I don't advise a career in smoking. My apologies, Philip Morris.

The bottom line is earning a living is work. Combining

hobbies and work still results in WORK.

I know some of you might love to entertain. A few of my friends certainly do. It's loads of fun, a lovely pastime one might relish once or twice a week. Perhaps you even send out those quaint calligraphy invites. Try entertaining friends and strangers twice a day at your home for months on end and see how much you like it. We can't all be Martha Stewart, dashing off to oversee a gardening tutorial in between arranging a hundred guest four-course meal. (Let's not kid ourselves; you know that behind that mother-of-the-year smile, she's crying inside, wishing she were still in jail.)

Sidebar #1: I have even been fooled into thinking I might like a job in areas that interest me on a very basic level. I'm going to give you a few examples, chronologically.

When I was a kid, I enjoyed math. It was like figuring out little puzzles and then I was granted the satisfaction of being right. Applied to the real world, I could compare it to winning an argument against a person I loathe. But as a child, solving easy math problems was a perfect way to retreat into a land of personal fulfillment.

Arithmetic seemed clear-cut and perfect. Not at all similar to life, which was a jagged entity, dependent on the changing aspects of each day's adventures. *Twenty-seven divided by three equals nine.* How neat and tidy! It was the same cool feeling as grooving at a nightclub, nodding your head in approval when a rap song rhymed perfectly.

Geometry – connecting the dots and drawing pictures. It didn't feel like learning, and I still don't know how it applies to life situations, but I liked it.

Algebra brought in the addition of the mysterious letter to every equation, but it was relatively simple and fun.

Then senior year in high school, everything changed. AP Calculus was my first taste of realizing some hobbies were not worth pursuing. Most equations led to a frustrating fraction that didn't look so clear cut at all. My answer would turn out to be 4.432,903 over 101 squared, and it wasn't even close to being correct. What was rewarding about that?

Math and I became brutal enemies. My mother's dangerous-looking Russian friend tutored me four times a week after school, to no avail. I struggled, worked, slaved, cursed, panicked, and sweated bullets to earn that F plus. *What the fuck is an F plus? A failing grade with a smiley face?*

I gave up all hope of becoming a math professor. My life just became one giant word problem instead. It boiled down to: how long will it take me to find a job that pays me well for doing absolutely nothing?

Sidebar #2: Eventually I found a college to accept me, despite an F in senior year math. Entering college, I was stupidly still flirting with all my hobbies as potential real life flings. I changed my major four times, as short-lived fads continued to rear their ugly heads.

The first major I chose was art therapy, modeled strictly after my "hobby" of drawing in pen and ink. (Commonly referred to as doodling.) Well, yes, I enjoyed drawing and painting, and still do, but no, it was not a good career move. Furthermore, I hated memorizing useless facts about dead painters. I also had no real desire to teach others how to express themselves through art. I just wanted to be left alone to paint my own pictures without having to talk to anyone. (See Chapter 16 for more on this.)

I nixed that major early, deciding I'd rather have a career in filmmaking. Again, NOT PRACTICAL. After taking all my required courses, I realized creating movies was much different that I'd imagined. It came down to a lot of long, tedious hours in an editing room. *Making movies was a pain in the ass!* Fooled again, I realized I just liked *watching* movies. This was an awful revelation to arrive at after three years of college.

Piggybacking onto another hobby, I thought I'd try my luck with the theater. All my friends were actors, I figured what the hell? Once again, I should have kept my hobbies separate from my career path. The fourth year of college is a little late to change your major to acting. It was dumber than I even realized, especially since I had no formal training and no idea of the politics involved.

In addition, I'd never read an entire play in my whole life and I felt Shakespeare might as well have been written in Portuguese. Playing Cinderella in my eighth grade play was not sufficient preparation for a future in the entertainment world. I soon learned that auditioning for a part in a serious Elizabethan play was a ridiculous waste of time. I had no interest in getting any professional training and wasn't up for the continual rejection I'd receive without it. Nine years later, I had to admit to myself that I didn't have the determination to make it any further than being part of an appreciative audience.

Midway through what was supposed to be my last year in college, I looked down at the true crime novel I was reading and thought, *I've been reading these books my whole life. I rent documentaries on hideous crimes and scandals to satisfy my own obscure curiosity. I have officially missed my calling.* After further reflection, I realized I should be a criminologist or maybe just a criminal. I added another major to my already full calendar.

It took me an extra year, but I finally graduated with a degree in media studies (concentration in theater – so fucking stupid) and sociology (concentration in crime – worthwhile.) I bet no one else has such a bizarre mix of useless knowledge floating around in their head. But, guess what, useless knowledge is fabulous to draw upon when you're pretending to be doing something.

Upon graduation I felt rather content, like I was on track. It wasn't clear what track exactly, but there was hope I wouldn't wind up homeless in a gutter somewhere, still searching for a career path.

That encouraging feeling didn't last long. Following my passion for crime, I landed a three-month internship at the Department of Investigation in downtown Manhattan. After three months, I was miserable, broke, and discouraged. There was also no excitement to be gained from working nine-to-five, five days a week, knee-deep in paperwork.

At the Department of Investigation, I was assigned to a division that investigated housing corruption in the five boroughs of New York City. The most exciting days I had were when I begged to go on location with some of the "detectives." These guys were not Lucas Davenport or Alex Cross, and trust me when I tell you, they had no air of mystery about them. Tagging along with them, however, was still better than pretending to fill out reports all day.

On "location," I'd sit in a car in front of various decrepit buildings in the South Bronx, waiting for some crack addict landlord to show his face. Far from exciting. Half the time the guy didn't even show. The image of myself as a high-profile investigator deflated in front of my eyes. True crime books glorify everything and make you feel like you're cracking a case single-handedly. In real life, it's just a lot of paperwork on boring misdemeanor crimes.

Occasionally, there were audiotapes that had to be transcribed. I couldn't hear shit, but I still opted for this chore over data entry because I could put my own music into the tape recorder from 1976, and no one knew the difference. Of course, I still had to produce, so I started making up interesting incriminating evidence that read well on paper. I'm sure they double-checked my work; I mean, who would trust me, a young girl fresh out of college who drank multiple strawberry daiquiris at the South Street Seaport during her lunch hour?

During this excruciating reality check, I found relief in my carefree, stupid waitress job at Fashion Café. Who would have thought? Nothing I did really mattered, and the money was better. Go figure. I could get drunk, talk to people, walk around, eat, and skip home with cash in my pocket. Far more than I was making at the Department of Investigation. My college education began to seem even less worthwhile. It still is. Twenty-four years later, I'm staring at this computer completely dumbfounded. Thank God, I found solace in embracing my key concepts, the exceptions to the rules: having sex, drinking, eating and smoking.

Sidebar #3: I got fired from the Department of Investigation when they eventually realized I was not taking the job seriously. (For investigators, it took them long enough.) I began tending bar full time, while I continued to pursue acting. I had a feeling "doing nothing" would eventually take top priority, but I wasn't completely sure until many years later when I attempted to go back to school for nutrition. We discussed this ridiculous subject already. (Refer back to Chapter 5 if your memory is failing you.) I mentioned it also had a two-hour lab attached to it, once a week for ten weeks. In this lab we had to cook. At that point in time, I had zero experience in the kitchen other than eating raw cookie dough.

It was then I realized I had a problem: unhappy with my own hobbies that I tried to turn into careers, I resorted to poaching other people's hobbies, thinking I could make a go of it. After all, I had a few friends who adored cooking!

In my confused state of mind – this was way before my mother discovered the abandoned food diary on my dirty kitchen floor – I figured if no one would hire me as their nutritionist, I could be a personal chef. I already knew from waiting tables that a cook or chef worked his ass off in a restaurant, but perhaps they didn't work so hard if they just cooked for one person? Or a family of two?

"Amy Minty. Chef to the Stars." At the time, I envisioned the headline with confidence. After all, I'd always enjoyed *eating* gourmet meals and *reading* recipes. What could be so hard about the actual cooking? Maybe I could apply my love of painting and frost cakes with artistic flair, I imagined, getting quite carried away.

Yep, it just goes to show, you never stop learning in life. This one stupid lab at NYU completely wiped out any far-fetched ideas of becoming a personal chef. Or a cook of any sorts.

After the first lab, I dreaded those two hours once a week. Cooking hadn't even made it to the level of a hobby before I rejected it.

Sidebar #4: In the field of nutrition, apparently, it's important to know why specific foods create particular responses in people. Hence, it's critical to be able to prepare these certain foods in a fashion suitable for a person with a specific ailment or food phobia. *Ugh,* I thought, sighing with the effort that might entail.

There I was, dressed in my culinary gear – one could have confused me with a pupil of martial arts – testing the effects of salt and lemon and vinegar on boiled carrots. This was labeled watching chemical balances occur in food over a monitored period of time. I labeled it bullshit. Like I cared at which moment the carrot disintegrated.

I was so bored. Cooking involved timing, careful measuring, endless stirring, and so much preparation. And temperature was important – I'd had no idea! It's so technical really, like engineering or architecture. Really fucking precise. That was the moment I realized one must know what he or she is doing in order to achieve the desired result. That took all the fun out of it for me.

To this day, as it did back then, the food channel makes cooking look easy because every single ingredient is already washed and cleaned and blanched for the chefs to juggle before swiping in mid-air with Wusthof knives. I don't know about you, but when the slivers of perfectly ripe tomatoes all land neatly in an All-Clad sauté pan, I'm highly suspicious.

At any rate, I learned that *watching* cooking is easier than manipulating the food to taste good. I spent the remaining nine lab sessions contemplating how to steal the entire supply of nuts and dried fruit from the dry goods storage.

Sure enough, I found myself hanging out at a Mexican bar called "Gonzalez Gonzalez," during my two-hour break between the horrid nutrition class and the lab. It was absolutely crucial that I capitalized on that time to unwind. A couple of strong margaritas before lab made it slightly more bearable. I just had to watch myself with the hot surfaces. One day, I leaned on a hot plate and my cooking jacket started burning. I immediately concluded that I'd caught on fire and proceeded to stop, drop, and roll on the ground in front of twenty other students. I was a legend from that day on. Too bad YouTube was still in its early stages.

Before the final exam, I attempted to stay out of the bar, but really, what else was there to do for two hours? *It wasn't like I could study for a lab test.* So . . . I went for a couple frozen drinks before the big exam. I remember this day clearly because dirty banana rum cocktails were on special so I switched it up. The weather was getting warmer, and I felt rather festive!

When I showed up for the lab on time for once, much to my surprise, everyone was already wearing their white cooking jackets, hard at work. It actually looked like I was surveying a culinary class of reckoning. Not exactly the Culinary Institute of America, but whatever. My stomach lurched, and I felt like an outsider wandering the halls in search of a restroom. This added to my rather low self-esteem at the time. At that precise second, I realized I truly did not belong there.

I tiptoed through the doorway and reached in my backpack for my burnt chef's jacket and knife, wondering if my watch had stopped after the second dirty banana. At that moment, Cecilia, my teacher, came flying at me through the door. *Cecilia, you're breaking my heart. I'm down on my knees, I'm begging you please...* Every time I saw her I started to hum. She must have noticed my appalled expression regarding the other students, because she burst into apology, "Amy, please, don't worry – you're not late!"

"Why would I think that?"

"Since it's the last day, I let everyone start early. You missed my announcement when you left the first class before anyone else."

"How early?" I squeaked.

"Oh, just an hour or so. Now, let's get you started."

I forced a smile. I saw three of her. I shoved some gum in my mouth.

"Now, here's your final assignment," she continued. I didn't yet know what ingredients I'd be working with for my final exam, which was fine with me. I liked it better that way because it cut down on wasting my time practicing or preparing. As if. "You're responsible for preparing a meat, it can be chicken also, a potato any style, except baked, and a green vegetable of your choice. When you're done, I'll sample the food and assign you your grade. I've asked that there be no talking between students during this time. Get to work!" She took off in the direction of the other room. As she turned, I dropped the obligatory smile, understanding too well how difficult it was to cheat under these circumstances.

I buttoned my karate jacket in the moment of truth. I was fucked. I cursed my potential hobby and walked sullenly to my cooking station. I took out my notebook, glancing for any tips I might have jotted down in the last nine classes. No notes. Only a few good drawings of Cecilia. Then a brilliant idea struck me. From the dark recesses of my mind, I remembered how to fry! I'd watched my mother fry everything in our largest pot growing up. All I needed was a couple of eggs and some breadcrumbs. Since I'd spotted breadcrumbs in the dry storage plotting my heist of the dried goods, I knew I'd be fine. I could make the fried platter! I set off to work.

While searching the Sub-Zero walk-in cooler for eggs, I spotted my lab partner. I'd never liked her. Despite the no-talking rule, she announced she was making a prosciutto omelet with Meyer lemon sour cream and an authentic avocado dip. I frowned and almost asked her about the potato, but knowing her, I suspected she'd already perfected a vichyssoise and it was simmering nearby. Grabbing the eggs, I rolled my eyes and stormed out.

I put all three items in the same burning hot oil to cut down on time. It seemed to work in my favor, since I completed my project before my hateful lab partner and most of the class. I attributed that to my speedy knowledge of where all the ingredients were located. I had basically canvassed the joint since I was planning to dash with a majority of the more expensive delicacies on my way out.

Fifteen minutes later, I'd created fried chicken nuggets (not of a marketable McDonald's quality, obviously), extremely large french fries (less cutting), and fried squash. Forgetting the vegetable was supposed to be green, the orange squash had been a gamble since I wasn't too familiar with vegetables unless they were sizzling in my fajita.

It came time for Cecilia to grade my "meal." I probably should have been nervous, but I wasn't. I guess one only feels nervous if they actually give a shit. I stood impatiently behind three other students holding their finished products, thinking mine wouldn't lend well to waiting. My turn finally came and I sat down opposite Cecilia at the table. She was writing something in her notebook before she looked up. I glanced down at my fried platter that was oozing grease through the paper plate, regretting my decision to fry everything in peanut oil.

Cecilia surveyed my plate of food. "Oh, Amy, everything looks . . . very oily, but I'm sure it tastes excellent. Tell me exactly what you made and how you prepared it."

This is when the lying comes in, I thought. I was hot as fuck and longing for some water.

I cleared my throat. "I present you with square chicken nuggets, intentionally oversized french fries, and large chunks of unidentified squash. I think it's of the acorn species. I know you told me to use a green vegetable, but I have a color recognition problem."

"I see," Cecilia said, picking up a fry the size of a biscotti cookie. She quickly placed it back down on the plate again. "How did you prepare the chicken?" she asked, switching her focus.

"In classic White Castle style – I assume you're familiar – I cut the chicken into squares, dipped them in egg yolk and rolled them in breadcrumbs before throwing them in the fryer."

"Did you rinse the chicken first?"

"Sure did." She knew I was lying. I liked her for not calling me on it. I started humming her song. *Cecilia, your breaking my heart . . .*

"You're not supposed to," she said lightly.

I truly cursed my latest and last hobby.

"Washing meat can cause bacterial growth if it's not cooked immediately after washing," she scolded.

"Yeah, but *Cecilia*, I did cook it immediately. I cooked it faster than a fisherman can throw a reject fish back into the ocean."

She just looked at me. "I'm regretting the fact this college is so progressive. The dean has urged me to be on a first name basis with my students, and I'm not sure how comfortable I am with this."

I shrugged. "I'm not your employer. At least not yet. Try the chicken nuggets."

She eyed me suspiciously and bit into a square nugget. I prayed it was cooked.

"Not bad," she said. "Did you prepare the squash

the same way?"

"Yep. Fries too! Killed three birds with one stone."

"Different oils, I hope?"

"You bet." I hoped the squash didn't taste mysteriously like chicken and french fries.

She sampled the squash. "What temperature did you cook this at?" she asked, wrinkling her nose.

Temperature? I smiled. *Why was that important for something fried?* "Does it taste OK?" I asked, avoiding the question.

"The oil should have been hotter. That would have given you a crispier result. I don't eat much fried squash, but I think it could have been better prepared."

"I don't know what that means," I said, looking at my watch. Gonzalez Gonzalez closed at eleven p.m. *And after today, I'll never have to cook anything again,* I thought. Little did I know what was in store for me in the year 2020.

"OK, I'm giving you a C for overall taste, an A for originality, and a D for presentation."

Presentation – shit! It was an NYU undergraduate class. I wasn't chef de cuisine at the Four Seasons. I suppose, I could have thrown some parsley on the plate or a slice of beet for color. It simply never occurred to me. *Good thing I'd ditched that art major.*

I averaged the three grades quickly in my head, arriving at PASSED! I was thrilled. At least I'd ruled out another possible hobby as a career. Its transformation into anything lucrative would have been virtually impossible, considering my inadequate skills and limited interest.

The moral of this chapter, in case I haven't been clear, is that you should never consider a hobby anything more than a pleasant pastime. Work is work, no matter how you look at it. Focus on finding a job that lets you get away with doing less. Get paid – do nothing! If you have one of these jobs, then you're in good shape. For the rest of us, sneak in a hobby at work and receive a paycheck while knitting that next scarf or betting blackjack online.

CHAPTER 8

Part 1

The Occasional Snags To Doing Nothing

I've been putting off this chapter because I didn't want to say anything negative about doing nothing. That is why it is chapter eight, and not chapter two. Unfortunately, once in a while, there can be drawbacks to doing nothing. You might find this hard to believe, but I'm only telling you in order to prepare you for run-ins with snags. In order for you to trust me, I must present you with all of the facts.

A snag is a person who wants to strike up conversation with you for no good reason. On top of being annoyingly outgoing and opinionated, this person never gets the hint that you would rather be left alone. A snag can be male or female, each capable of ruining your solitude. A snag can be singular or there can be groups; sometimes they travel in packs. Alone, or with others, snags are always irritating. In time, if you keep reading, you will become a pro at dodging them.

Being hounded by a snag happens to everyone on occasion. It's important to stay grounded and defend your unique independence when a snag strikes. I'd much rather be a complete snob than a pathetic sucker stuck talking to an annoying geek about the deep web just for the hell of it. Those who do nothing have better things to do!

Many years ago, before I made "doing nothing" my top priority, I found myself getting caught in difficult positions with snags. I continuously succumbed to pointless conversations, offering free advice to people I'd never see again. I was left feeling frustrated and used.

What is the point of having bullshit conversations with strangers? These snags just want to worm their way into our lives. Is there a reason we should stand there and chat with others that we really don't care about and sometimes dislike on sight? I think not. Sure, we don't want to see them gunned down in front of our eyes, but what's the expression – *out of sight, out of mind?*

Depending on your lifestyle, you might have had the unlucky experience of going on a blind date. Nine times out of ten, the man or woman will be a snag. Snags love opportunities to get to know more people. They thrive on it. Snags also adore computer dating and place exaggerated advertisements online in an attempt to "sell" themselves. Beware.

Being stuck talking to a snag used to make me angry. I could have been reading a book instead of exerting valuable energy. Then I realized it was my own fault. If we don't protect ourselves, then ultimately, we're welcoming the intrusion.

Please understand that not everyone you meet for the first time will be a snag. There are still a few nice people out there that you simply haven't met yet. Some will even wind up becoming close friends. Do not worry about clarifying a distinction between this cool new person and a snag. It will be painfully obvious immediately whether they fall into the "I'm going to attempt to bug the shit out of you" category. Save your energy for people you enjoy being around.

I encourage most people to cross over into the world of doing nothing. That's what I believe in, and I wouldn't change my advice under any circumstances. But, again, we who excel in living this perfect nirvana are sometimes the prime targets for moronic snags.

For instance, you might be outside enjoying the day or loitering inside a store when a stranger decides he or she would like to get to know you. God, it's like fighting off gnats in the woods when you're trying to enjoy the scenery. Suddenly the emptiness of your apartment or house seems like your best bet.

There are a few places where you definitely have to be more careful. Some locations just ooze snags. Abide by these basic rules.

- Avoid airplanes, buses and trains. (And I was saying this well before COVID-19 reared its ugly head.) Public transportation can be a bitch so stay clear of carpools, minivans, and shuttle buses while on vacation. It's hard to find a more determined snag than a tourist traveling alone. Opt for a cab instead. It's worth the extra money.

- Never stay at a friend's house for an extended period of time unless you're secretly in love with him or her, or you know for a fact that they will never pose a problem. I recommend at least a five-year grace period of knowing them well. Casual acquaintances often turn into snags if you overstay your welcome.

- Do not stay with relatives, even if they insist. Take comfort in knowing they feel obligated to offer their hospitality because they're related to you. Chances are, they would prefer you stayed in a nearby hotel. (As would you!)

- Do not hang for extended periods of time in places of worship. It's OK to practice your religion, but if you're just pretending to be religious, stay clear. Religious fanatics can spot a faker in a crowd, and they will stalk you until you reform. If you're not the least bit spiritual, a lecture on religion from a snag could turn you into an atheist.

- Don't tend bar. First of all, it's too much work. Second, no one can help you if you're stuck behind that bar on a slow night. Make no mistake about it, you are trapped. The combination of annoying and drunk snags just might put you over the edge. At least if you're waiting tables, you can walk away.

Keep alert for snags when you enter into a park, historical landmark, or campground (which you should avoid anyway – see Chapter 13 on vacationing). Too many people hang out at these places that don't appreciate the art of doing nothing. They want to meet people and have stimulating conversations regarding the view or the weather. Always be on the lookout; it's easier to avoid snags if you can spot them coming.

- Stay out of tourist attractions. This one should be obvious. Come on! Keep away from Planet Hollywood unless you're surrounded by bodyguards. There are too many single travelers with nothing to do. The ones that don't know any better will arrive at the tourist trap looking for someone to talk to. Put it this way: anyone who's actually interested in seeing the Statue of Liberty alone is going to be the first one to try and strike up a conversation with you.

If a snag happens to sneak up on you, it's important to be able to identify him or her quickly. Immediately, act busy. Look positively consumed with something – anything! You don't actually have to be doing much to appear busy. The following devices are excellent props to keep with you at all times:

♦ Earbuds or Any Type of Headphones

This is your finest tool, even if your batteries are dead. It is the true conversation stopper and clearly conveys you want nothing to do with the person. When a snag begins to speak, you can slide your earbuds into your ears. It's rude, but so what? We're not trying to befriend snags anyway.

♦ Books that Raise Red Flags

I know a good one. It's called *Surviving the Flesh-Eating Bacteria*. These two brave authors just came out with a second edition. The title is in bold print. No one, crazy or not, wants to take that risk.

Books on certain subjects like *Famous Mass Murders* and *The Big Book of Serial Killers* can also be helpful in scaring off people. If you've attracted a real nut case, however, you might be making things worse for yourself. Analyze the person before casually slipping it out of your bag.

♦ A Cell Phone

These days most people are glued to their cellphones, but that wasn't always the case. I remember making the switch from my beeper to a huge portable device that only worked with D batteries. Thank God for technology. Now we can pre-set an alarm to go off at the mere sighting of a snag. If you anticipate a problem, you can just pretend it vibrated, claiming a tiger is loose in your neighborhood.

♦ Mace

This is a super prop to have with you at all times. It shows you're hyper aware of your whereabouts and are prepared to protect yourself in the big city.

Keep in mind, chefs get to carry knives, dentists get to carry drills, carpenters get to carry chainsaws and policemen get to carry guns. You can at least give the impression of power. Why should we be left out just because we're not doing anything?

Sidebar: Here is an example of a brief encounter I had dealing with riffraff. This particular confrontation took place at one of my lovely jobs many years ago. It was one of those annoying nights when I was forced to make an effort. Right there, that put me in a bad mood. I had just finished explaining to my manager that we needed to hire barbacks that could tell the difference between dirty glasses and clean. We servers were getting tired of pointing out the difference.

I was at my station by the bathrooms, pissed off that I had to concentrate. In the middle of entering a table's order into the computer, this customer snuck up behind me and attempted to start a conversation. I looked over my shoulder and realized it was the same jerk that asked me if we carried Mad Dog. (Like I work at the supermarket.)

"So what do you really do?" he asked me. I rolled my eyes. If there was one question I couldn't stand, that would be the one. It never occurs to thickheaded people that night jobs are still full-time jobs. It's a double insult.

"None of your business. And it's rude to ask personal questions to a stranger," I added.

"You're not a stranger. You're our waitress."

"Same thing, buddy."

"No, really. What do you do?" he persisted.

I spun around, eyes flaring. "I'm the Northeast regional director for Kentucky Fried Chicken."

"Ha, ha. What are you? An actress?"

"I also oversee all mashed potato production for

Boston Market. But just in the United States, not globally."

He finally looked confused.

"Yeah. I work three jobs so that's why I don't feel like answering your dumb fucking questions."

That sort of shut him up. I was at work, so I had to make do without most of my props. He turned to his friend waiting with him by the bathroom and said, "I think the waitress is mad at me."

"No kidding," the friend agreed, "Leave her alone, man. Would you want to work here?" The moron's buddy was clearly a decent guy stuck with a snag for a friend.

Luckily, I was done with ringing in my order and could walk away. That is the only way to handle a situation like that. Just lie until they know you're lying. This signifies they will never get to know you. Remember you're in charge. If you feel like talking for no reason, then by all means, go right ahead. But if you don't, stick up for yourself. You have the principle of "doing nothing" behind you!

CHAPTER 8

Part 2

The More Serious Snag: Law Enforcement

This may seem an odd topic for the people universally trying to do nothing, but you might be surprised. Doing nothing naturally draws attention to you because of the laws of nature. Basically, you don't always get what you want; hence, when you are minding your business, longing to be left alone, you usually attract problems.

In your newly adjusted mindset of doing nothing, you are nonchalant and happy, free of the constant worries that plague your life. Perhaps you're walking around in a carefree mood, enjoying a spring day, while sipping a cold Coors Light from a paper bag. You probably look so relaxed sitting there on that park bench in Midtown, watching all those uptight businessmen scurry to their offices that, naturally, you become a target for those who are jealous.

Some people are so wigged-out and panicked they don't even notice you. That's the only type you like. It's the others you need to be careful of. Law enforcement, in particular, hates your smug smile, as you lick your ice cream and read your newspaper. I'll give you an example . . .

Sidebar: Many years ago, I was walking down Third Avenue on my way to a movie. I had some tunes cranking in my Sony Walkman and my dark sunglasses on, so I had no peripheral vision. I was drinking Landshark beer from a brown paper bag. Excited to see *Heartbreakers*, a movie about a mother/daughter team of con artists, I was walking a little faster than my normal stroll. However, because of my cool shades and the music blaring, I didn't hear or see the policeman sneak up behind me. I was in mid-step when this hazy creature clad in black polyester pulled my earphones down around my neck. It was so rude! All I heard was "Miss!" Apparently, he'd been trying to get my attention.

I stopped, removed my shades, and peered at him. He was very pale with the lightest shade of blond hair – not always becoming on a guy. He even had one of those cowlicks you see in cartoons.

"Did I drop something?" I asked innocently, fully aware I wasn't carrying anything but my drink.

"What's in the bag, miss?" he asked.

"Snapple?"

"I didn't know they made Snapple in a longneck bottle. May I see it?" he asked.

"Did I say Snapple? I meant beer."

"Do you know it's against the law to have an open container of liquor on a public street?" he asked.

"I didn't know that, sir." *Who doesn't know that?*

Where I'm from, they warn you about that in kinder-garten.

"Well, you should know by now," he scowled. Now he resembled a duck, but not the cute kind.

"How come I always see homeless people drinking from a bottle of Jack then?" I asked, glancing at my watch.

"It's still illegal," he argued. "Do you have any ID on you? You don't even look old enough to be drinking."

"I'm twenty-seven," I said, pulling out my New York Sports Club card. I was going to be late for the movie, and I was getting annoyed.

"Anything with a birth date on it?" he asked, looking suspiciously at the cheap piece of plastic. I knew I didn't have anything on me, of all days. Which was stupid, since my mother was always telling me to carry identification so if I got hit by a bus and died, she'd be notified. I pulled out the other card I had in my back pocket. It was a Blockbuster card, and I didn't bother to show it to Howard the Duck.

"Sir, I left my ID at home. I'm on my way to a movie," I added, hoping he'd realize I was on an important schedule.

"Tell ya what. I'm going to take away the beverage and just give you a warning because you didn't know it was illegal," he scoffed.

Beverage? Who still uses that word? I thought it went out with Prohibition. He finally let me go on my merry way. I was lucky he wasn't a real prick, but I still missed the movie previews. The lesson to be learned here is always carry ID. Most places are not as relaxed as New Orleans when it comes to walking around wasted off your ass.

Also, make sure to carry your beer down if you're not swigging from it. It's even better if you can keep it hidden in your purse upright. If you want to be really safe, make your own homemade punch and stick it in a cranberry juice bottle. 151 Rum is a really good value these days now that it's not so popular.

The second important lesson to remember is similar to the first. Always carry your ID on you when you go to a bar or club, especially after four o'clock in the morning when the sale of liquor is prohibited. I learned this the hard way.

Sidebar #2: Still in my twenties, I was at an after-hours place (an establishment that stays open after it's supposed to be shut) one early morning after work. It was located on the fourth floor of a random building in the garment district. I was having a good time relaxing at the bar with some friends when an entire SWAT team, fully equipped with machine guns, raided the place.

Well, that was a major pain-in-the-ass, having to keep my hands up against a wall for two hours while they frisked a hundred and fifty people for drugs and weapons. They even took away my wine key. I told them I was a waitress, and they just shoved me against the wall and confiscated it.

It turned out the after-hours joint had been under serious surveillance for months due to drug-trafficking, gambling, prostitution, money laundering and the sale of liquor after four a.m. It hadn't felt particularly dangerous, and I had even made a few bucks at the roulette table so I didn't see what all the fuss was about. Not to mention I'd been frequenting the place at least once a week since it opened.

The militant bunch of cops made us wait until they took everyone's personal information. Those without ID were dragged down to a Bronx police station to be fingerprinted.

Thankfully, I'd had ID on me, so I didn't have to pay the hundred-dollar fine. It was bad enough I didn't get home until nine thirty in the morning. I crawled into bed, vowing to stay away from after-hours establishments. That vow lasted until they opened up at their new location.

Cops will also try and get you for what they deem might endanger others. While you may be doing something that feels good for you, they label it "causing a disturbance." I'll give you another example from my personal life.

Sidebar #3: In November of 2000, I quit another terrible job. It was another winner restaurant that should probably go unnamed, but what do I care? It was called Candela, and it shut down after I left anyway.

At this stage, I was twenty-six and not a stranger to stupid, uptight, restaurant environments, but this place was the absolute worst. I only worked there for four months, and in that time, I did everything in my power to get fired. Half of the time I didn't show up, and I wouldn't even bother to call with some lame excuse. I had something like nine warnings.

The uniform was obscene. The enormous button down, maroon shirt came down to my knees if I didn't tuck it into my very corporate black pants. Worn together with a long, yellow apron, I looked like a cross between a beet and a banana. About an hour into my shift, I decided I couldn't wear it a second longer, and walked out the door.

I raced out of there leaving all my tables wondering where their food was. I bounced merrily along Sixteenth Street and turned north onto Park Avenue, tearing off the apron as I went. It was made with that nasty polyester material that you can't rip without the help of a chainsaw. Realizing it was practically indestructible, I reached for my lighter, stepped over the nearest metal trashcan, and proceeded to light it on fire. It took to flame much better than I assumed it would, and pretty soon the entire trash can was ablaze. It looked like I was in charge of a book-burning riot. On the edge of Gramercy Square Park, the center for anti-establishment protests, it wouldn't have been out of the question.

Now these were the days before 9/11 rocked our nation and changed our lives forever. I wouldn't do this in today's world. But even back then, it didn't take long for two policemen to notice me about to flee the scene.

As the cops approached me, one two feet taller than the other, I quickly labeled them Tall and Small.

"Are you responsible for this fire?" Small asked. It seemed like they were both trying not to laugh. In order for them to exchange giggles, Small had to look up and Tall had to look down. It was hard to take them seriously.

I wondered for a split second if I could get in real trouble, but I calmed myself. *People probably do stuff like this all the time*, I thought. "Yep," I said, finally answering them. "I just quit the worst job of my life and the only appropriate thing to do was burn the uniform."

They looked at me like I was crazy. Maybe I was. I watched the flames. The fire was no longer so big; luckily there hadn't been much trash in the can. I could tell that Small and Tall were still assessing how dangerous I might be.

"Try not to do this again, ma'am," Small said, "This fire could have endangered others."

"Yeah, OK," I said. "But if you ever worked at that restaurant," I continued, pointing at Candela in the distance, "you'd understand."

Fortunately for me, their little radios went off in tandem, and they let me off the hook. It was lunchtime, so Small and Tall probably needed to secure their table at Stuff-a-Bagel.

Amy Minty

Just in case it isn't clear, starting a fire in the middle of Park Avenue is an example of what NOT to do. I have somehow avoided getting arrested in my lifetime, but I'm only forty-seven. There is still time.

CHAPTER 9

Sports and Other Activities

I encourage light exercise for all ages because, according to popular belief, it's good for us. Supposedly, it provides stress relief and aids in getting proper rest at night. Keeping that in mind, it's worth discussing. Do not forget, I said "light" activity – no marathons.

Do I like to exercise? No. I'd rather be watching TV or reading a book. However, I have found from my own level of personal experience that if I just watch TV all day, I can't sleep at night. I suppose it makes sense. If I haven't exerted the slightest bit of energy all day long, why would my body feel it was time to rest?

Hence, people need to do something in order to keep a little blood flowing through our veins. I tend to lean toward sports you can do by yourself. This has nothing to do with the global pandemic, albeit it should. It's because most people annoy me, and I prefer the sound of my own thoughts when I'm forcing myself to exercise. To give you an example, rowing a boat by myself in a small stream would be more appealing to me than whitewater rafting down a waterfall with a bunch of crazy lunatics from New Zealand.

Below, I've outlined a few examples of sports that enhance doing nothing and I follow it up with sports to avoid. I recommend the following activities to those who want to get solid sleep at night without posing too much risk to their body.

♦ Walking

It's kind of fun to stroll along with absolutely no destination in mind other than the candy store. You can listen to music without your earbuds falling out from too much movement. Avoiding snags and other people is also much easier when your body is in motion. Not to mention, walking is much safer than standing in the middle of the sidewalk looking around. You're less likely to be confused with a straggling tourist. (Although, with people wearing masks, the distinction between tourists, snags and cool people minding their own business is getting harder to determine at first glance.)

If you're walking in a city, you get to see all the new restaurants and bars that have crept up around you while you were sleeping. If you have a keen eye, you'll notice the billboards looming above you. Advertising can be inspiring! Hence, walking in a city leads to shopping! And, obviously, I don't mean supermarket shopping. You can also walk around in the country or the suburbs, but you won't be able to shop as much unless you live on that one hip block with the Target and the Stop & Shop. It can still be fun if you're brave enough to chance walking along a highway. If you're lucky, you might stumble across a mall!

The prospect of getting injured while walking is relatively low as long as you look before crossing the street. If you're walking after dark, I recommend staying clear of parks and playgrounds. If I were broke, homeless, and desperate, those are the first places I'd seek out.

♦ Golf

Remember watching Bob Hope on the golf course in his golden years? He lived to be a hundred, and he was born in 1903, before we even had decent medicine! He was never a football player raging down a field, crashing head first into his opponents. He just putted away. He should be an inspiration to us all.

Golf allows you plenty of fresh air, minimal walking (if you're smart enough to use a cart), and every few minutes you hit a ball as precisely as you can. Also, that little golf cart is a great place to store your cooler of drinks and snacks!

You can also enjoy lunch at the golf course restaurant and peruse the pro shop for cute golf skirts! Playing golf by yourself can be an excellent avenue for meeting potential dates with the same common interests as you. For anyone who never saw Richard Gere in *Dr. T. & the Women*, I highly recommend golf as a classy way to hit on someone. Just be careful not to behave like a snag. Having said that, be sure to also *avoid* golf snags. If you happen to get really good at golf, you might even make some money out of it. Email me directly for golf courses across the U.S. that provide the best opportunities for hustling.

On the golf course, however, beware of strange tan lines. Opt for tank tops rather than T-shirts. Otherwise, you will look stupid naked.

♦ Fishing (This does not include ice fishing – too cold!)

All you need is a fishing pole and a nearby bait and tackle store. You don't want to be digging for worms yourself. They also have this new artificial bait now that isn't slimy. The boat is really unnecessary, but definitely adds to the experience. Who needs fishing if you find yourself in a bathing suit on a sundeck, two-fisted and partying on the Intracoastal Waterway? Again, not a rowboat in some dirty canal. Think big, think yacht! Think the Riviera!

Back to fishing as a sport: If you have any desire to eat the fish you catch, I'd be careful of *where* you choose to fish. I have heard horror stories of contaminated sea creatures. People fishing in New York's East River should know better.

♦Swimming

There is one caveat: you must know how to swim. The lifeguard's job is difficult enough watching all those little tykes careen backwards off the diving board. He or she won't notice when you start gasping for air in the deep end. Especially in Florida. Good luck!

Now, please be clear that I do not mean "competitive" swimming. You do not need a cap and goggles to do the back float. You should not think of swimming in terms of a race. Imagine paddling in a pool in the Caribbean sipping your frozen Piña Colada from a colorful paper straw. Try not to flash back to your local, over-chlorinated, YMCA indoor pool, where the lifeguard's average age was eighty and he still felt compelled to wear a Speedo.

Sidebar: You may have noticed that I stuck strictly to pools when I discussed swimming for recreational purposes. Assuming that most of you have seen the movie Jaws, I will simply state that oceans are dangerous.

Once upon a time, in junior high, a couple friends and I all thought we were capable of challenging the waves off a New Hampshire coastline. In fact, I seem to remember it was my idea to see how far we could swim out past the ropes.

Before we knew it, we were out pretty damn far, whooping with laughter and high-fiving one another. After making fun of all the little specks down at the water's edge, we decided to head back. And head back and head back. That was the moment I realized my idea had not been so great after all. Those little specks were actually worried onlookers urging us back to land. We were all out of breath, and since we had just watched *Revenge of the Nerds 2: Nerds in Paradise* at the theater we kept quoting Lewis and Gilbert, stranded out at sea for seventy-two hours before they were rescued. Every two minutes one of us shouted "Seventy-two hours!" and struggled to stay afloat.

We still thought it was funny, until we realized the number of people at shore were growing exponentially. Some "specks" were bright orange in color. Up until that moment, I'd never known the sound of a lifeguard's whistle could carry so far.

We learned later that my friend's mother – the idiot who'd been stupid enough to take her kid's friends on vacation with them – had gone and fetched the Coast Guard. (If my mother had been in charge, she probably wouldn't have even noticed we were gone.) Any confidence the three of us had in our swimming ability prior to this excursion was suddenly not so high. We had to be rescued by boat. The three of us were all pruned and admittedly ashamed for venturing a quarter mile past the ropes.

Needless to say, we were driven home after that. I'm still not sure whether we were banned from Hampton Beach for life, or if our families decided to stick to shallow lakes for the next few years. I could go into many other examples of the hazard of oceans, but I think you get my point. Stick to wave pools in water parks. Trying not to drown is work!

◆ Watching Sports Live

Going to a sporting match is a great substitute for exercising. Being at a live baseball game can be almost like a bizarre form of aerobics. Lots of jumping up and down, pumping your fists in the air. It's even fun to fool people and let them think the game matters to you, especially when you don't know which color the home team is wearing.

Football and rugby games also inspire a lot of team spirit when it comes to watching people beat the crap out of each other. Boxing matches and hockey games are even better for that. I would say wrestling too, but honestly, it is so unappealing to watch the competitors squeezed into those unbecoming outfits. I'm not even going to comment on sumo wrestling.

I'm not sure if race car driving is considered a sport, or simply a dance with death, despite having seen that Tom Cruise movie ten times. However, it sure can elevate your heart rate watching all those accidents.

Attending a tennis match is really good for the neck muscles, but it's probably not the best for your ass. There isn't much jumping up and down in tennis.

♦ Betting on Sports

You will sweat watching those horses go around . . . and around. The more money you lay down, the better exercise it will be. If you win, you'll be doing jumping jacks! If you lose, you'll lose your appetite, which is the next best thing to not exercising.

♦ Bicycle Riding

Don't think triathlon. Don't even think roads. Think quiet indoor facility with stationary bikes. (Refer back to Chapter 1.) Gyms have plenty, and these bikes usually have cup holders for your soda or Pringles and magazine holders for your iPad. Gyms also have free WIFI so you can stream Netflix. It's totally worth the membership.

If you refuse to listen to me and insist upon buying an actual 10-speed bike, I hope you live in the countryside or near Central Park. Stick to shady trails without too many hills. Avoid biking on the beach and in the desert. Also make sure to get one of those great baskets! They might look dumb, but they're perfect for carrying snacks, cigarettes, and your props for avoiding snags. Although, be careful in some parts of New Jersey where deer are plentiful; they love to cross the street directly in front of bikes and cars. Bambi is not so graceful when she's wrapped around your handlebars.

♦ Any Exercise for Which There is an Infomercial

Suzanne Somers looked pretty good from only using that Thighmaster. Don't you think?

I can attest to the fact that most of the equipment for sale at two a.m. – or probably resale – is not going to get you huffing and puffing. It's either going to break, in which case you'll get your money back, or the sheer assembly of it will drive you to the nearest gym out of frustration.

A couple years ago, I ordered a piece of machinery off an infomercial. I was drunk and watching television in the wee hours of the morning. Somehow, my enthusiastic vodka-driven frame of mind inspired me to call up and purchase something called the Fitness Flyer. It arrived ten weeks later. At the time, I was single, so I paid my superintendent to put it together. I used it until I got sick of it, *like most things*, but it really wasn't bad. It was low-impact and you felt like you were skiing in the air. I used it until it broke; then I returned it and received a full refund. How can you go wrong?

♦ The Precor Elliptical Trainer

For those of you who have never heard of this monster of a machine, it's similar to the Fitness Flyer, but it's got a big motor. Honestly, using the machine is really easy. Most gyms have them and you just glide up and down effortlessly while you read from your Kindle.

Naturally, I can think of more minimal ways to exercise, but I've listed the best ones. It's much more important that you know which sports to avoid.

♦ Any Sports That Involve Cold Temperatures

For me, skiing in Vermont equates to drinking a lot of hot chocolate and never leaving the lodge. If a ski area can make man-made snow, that usually indicates its average temperature is bitterly cold. Freezing your ass off is definitely doing something. If you're foolish enough to go along with your family's idea of a good time, bring several books and be prepared to get comfortable in front of the fireplace.

This category also includes sledding, which can be truly dangerous if there are a significant number of trees at the bottom of the hill. Notice there are very few documented ways to steer a sled? Sleds do not take direction well.

What about ice skating? Risking your life in order to stay vertical is just plain stupid. Not to mention those ponds are sketchy. *How does one know if the ice is completely frozen?* Ice skating at an indoor rink is safer – and there are rails to hold onto – but it's still cold. Whenever I watch figure skating on TV, I feel a slight pang to give it a whirl, (no pun intended) but the logical part of my brain kicks in reminding me that I fall easily and often when the level ground below me is not even slippery.

Snowboarding is not an option, as being a champion surfer is a prerequisite. Do not attempt it under any circumstances unless you enjoy falling headfirst into cold, wet snow. This brings me to my next topic of disdain.

♦ Gymnastics and Diving

Have you seen the Olympics lately? I'm not even sure which category is the worst. It's like asking yourself in an airplane: Would I rather crash over land or water? The stress involved in gymnastics has to be greater than any other sport I can think of. Who can do a triple flip off a springboard and land on a balance beam successfully? Who's even willing to try? In my youth, I couldn't even get the cartwheel right.

Bottom line: The television coverage of these gymnastic competitions should have warnings on the bottom of the screen: DO NOT TRY THIS AT HOME. Not to mention, to compete in this sport you need to train ten hours a day starting at age four.

Diving is straight-up maniacal, but landing in twenty feet of water seems like it would be a better cushion for your head than a thin blue mat.

♦ Skydiving

Hahaha. As if? This is not a sport; this is a suicide attempt. That goes for bungee jumping and parachuting as well. Forget it. Even watching this "sport" on television can raise your blood pressure.

♦ Track and Long-Distance Running

The mere thought of this category is by far the most laughable. Who cares who can run the fastest fifty-yard dash in the world? Sprinting down the block is only an option if your significant other is chasing you.

♦ Sports That Look Easy

Trust me, synchronized swimming is a bitch. It's much harder than it appears. Those of you who haven't tried it, should, if only for comedic value. That being said, it's not the only sport meant to deceive us.

Did you know that in water polo, those men and women (clad almost always in blue and red) compete in the *deep* end of the pool? They're not standing in the shallow area while they score goals; they're keeping themselves afloat while they catch, throw, shoot and dunk each other. No thanks.

♦ Ice Hockey

On the same note, teams like the New York Rangers make ice hockey look easy. Don't forget that floor hockey takes skill, and that's just a game played in a gymnasium or a run-down tennis court with your fellow high school dropouts. In my case, I think we played it in the back parking lot of the Worcester Centrum. Real hockey is played on *ice*. Why?

♦ Sports You're Uncertain About

If you don't know what the sport entails, it's best to stay clear of it. Perhaps you've never heard of squash, but a new friend has thrown you a sweatband and invited you to play. Don't agree to reserve a court and assume it will be fun. You'll be in for a rude awakening.

♦ Soccer

Just say no. Refer back to the Track and Long-Distance Running category, as there are many similarities. Then add a ball to the mix—one you can't pick up with your hands and aggressively throw at one of your opponents. Whoever thought of a concept so stupid?

Sidebar: About thirty-five plus years ago, I was encouraged by my father to play soccer. Unbeknownst to me, he signed me up, then proceeded to drop me off at a large field where other little people were running around after a black and white checkered ball.

My key memory, besides not being very good at kicking, (weak ankles from too much lounging around) was that I was not motivated. Seriously now, what was my incentive?

I remember preferring to play defense. That way if my team's offense was good, I rarely had to move. I just let the goalie handle all the balls that got past me, which was all of them.

I also recall faking many injuries and watching from the bench a majority of the time while I held ice to my "injured" knee. I was not meant to play soccer. I could barely keep up in a game of neighborhood tag. To conclude, I advocate low risk, light energy sports. Professional athletes are not average human beings. We should compare them to action heroes like Super-woman or Batman.

CHAPTER 10
Doing Nothing At Starbucks And Other Neighborhood Locations

Oh, wow. Where do I begin? If you start to enjoy your life a little more by adhering to my helpful advice, you will be sure to have more time on your hands to do nothing at places outside your home. Coffee shops and restaurants are perfect places to settle in for a while and observe others. There are fewer people out and about to observe these days, but hopefully, we, as a world, will eventually regain a measure of normalcy. As always, there are two important rules to follow:

1. Never think about things you should be doing.
2. Always bring something to do, even if you have no intention of doing it. You never know when a snag is going to approach you. Remember your props.

After careful exploration of the perfect places to relax, I have found that Starbucks is by far the finest. Keep in mind, I'm not crazy about the fact they've taken over almost every street corner from Los Angeles to New York, but they still seem to maintain a steady stream of customers throughout the day. This high volume takes the emphasis off you as the consumer. You can blend in with others for hours, capitalizing on their property. To this day, I have never had to pay for office space.

One day, I spent thirteen hours in a Starbucks on the corner of Broadway and West Fourth Street. If I hadn't ordered absolutely everything on the menu and gone to the bathroom four times, they never would have known I was there. It's like becoming invisible without any special potion. (However, if you were invisible, there would never be any demands placed on you, making this book unnecessary.)

If, by some fluke, you don't live near a Starbucks, any local coffee shop in your area will usually do the trick. The busier the coffee shop the better, providing you can get a seat. Initially, you might think a slower-paced environment lends better to doing nothing, but it's actually the opposite. The high volume of people keeps you entertained, and the employees are too busy trying to look busy to notice you overstaying your welcome. (Since the pandemic, clearly, this theory has had undergone necessary changes.)

In places where the baristas and waiters have nothing to do, you can bet you're going to have to spend a minimum for every hour you're there. If there isn't a minimum, you'll need to get really good at ignoring the constant glares from behind the counter. Trust me, an employee in a slow coffee shop will get sick of the sight of you, but a decent tip will help your cause substantially. (Not only have I been that customer, I have also been that employee. My colleagues and I thought up names for people that lounge around all day long.) Employees also aren't keen on you taking up their best table for ten hours while you sip your tall, mocha, half-caf, skim milk latte with whipped cream and caramel drizzle.

Don't forget that loitering can also lead to the occasional fine, and cops breeze through a coffee shop about every half an hour to an hour on average, in just about every state. The staff can't complain about you if they don't have time to notice you. Hence, stick to Starbucks or busier coffee shops.

I happen to be at Starbucks right now as a matter of fact. (I wrote this segment back in December of 2019.) My "office" is beautifully busy. I am sitting to the left of two rather animated gentlemen, perfect examples of the lot you might encounter, and for which you should be prepared. These two individuals are South Florida's version of *Grumpy Old Men*. They're so confrontational with each other that if I couldn't see them, I'd swear it was Jack Lemmon and Walter Matthau arguing over their cappuccino and biscotti. In addition to being animated, they're actually rather informative. Since doing nothing most of the time tends to make you inquisitive, I overhear a lot. According to Jack and Walter, the mail service is not what it used to be in comparison to how it was in 1939. I didn't even know we had mail back then, and I can't believe it's not as efficient in today's world. I'm not sure if they have their facts straight, but they also claim there will be no mail delivered on Saturdays anymore in the near future. That sounds like good news to me. The less mail the better. Fewer bills and less correspondence with credit bureaus and debt collectors. Ultimately, less to worry about.

Next, they discussed the Internet. Did you know you could read the daily obituaries on the Web? That's a strange hobby. I guess at their age, it makes more sense. *Oh boy, they've spotted my computer. It's all over now.*

I'm back to report I was right. Walter noticed me first. "What kind of computer is that?" he demanded to know.

"It's a Mac Pro." I forced a smile and looked down at my plastic knife.

"Is that an Apple?" Jack asked, confused.

"Yes." I said, clearing my throat.

"Are you a college student?" Walter probed. "This place is crawling with them."

The kid reading a textbook next to me looked up sharply in his defense.

"I was a college student about twenty years ago," I answered. "Now I negotiate the sale of weapons to various military bases around the globe." It's fun to make up stories about yourself and tell them to people who don't matter. I began polishing the plastic knife with one of Starbuck's brown paper napkins, wondering if it could actually do some damage.

"Have you seen those new Apple laptops? Twenty-six hundred dollars, but boy are they worth it!" Walter cut in, not the least bit interested in my high-ranking, covert sales job.

"I have," I said sourly, glancing at my three-year-old computer. It figured they'd try to one-up me. How aggravating. I was supposed to be the young and trendy one while the older generation held on to the notion that typewriters were still the best medium for writing.

"Yeah, it's got a large, wide screen and weighs only five pounds!" he exclaimed, surreptitiously eyeing up my laptop.

My laptop is extremely heavy.

"And they look sharp and shiny with a battery that lasts

for ten hours!" he continued.

Fully charged, mine lasts three.

I put the plastic knife down and slid in my earbuds. "Sorry," I offered, "I have a conference call with the Department of Defense." It was clear they didn't believe me, but I didn't care.

Now Walter and Jack are gone, and I'm still here, listening to Pitbull. Can you believe that Walter and Jack left after just an hour? I'm not sure how long they were here before me, but if I were retired, I'd be milking it until I got hungry enough for real food.

Here is another interesting observation I just made: There are some people that would rather stand around looking clueless than sit at a dirty table. How stupid is that? There's a lady here next to me that stood in front of a dirty table for almost fifteen minutes until a Starbucks employee magically appeared. The lady stopped him in mid-step and asked him to clean it. God, like these employees don't have enough to do. Then the lady, whose name must be Rose, spread out a napkin over the seat before she sat down. Ridiculous! She then unfolded another napkin over the remarkably clean table before setting her plate down. You must be a skeptic if you doubt the powers of Windex. I killed a bug earlier today with Windex.

Rose even refused to put her strange array of belongings on the floor, opting for a chair instead, which she dragged from a nearby table. Rose must be either OCD, or she views Starbucks in the same category as the outdoor benches in North Philly. (Strangely enough, now it is almost a year later, and as I reread this segment, I'm realizing maybe Rose knew something I didn't. Interesting.)

See, I learn so much about people as I sit here doing nothing. I'm also giving others the very generous privilege of observing me! I'm looking around now, ready to exchange some knowing glances, but no one seems the least bit curious. Strange. I also have to force myself to look away from Rose, because if she slaps on gloves to eat her cookie, I might lose it.

That reminds me of my next point. While hanging out by yourself in a coffee shop, lounge, restaurant, or the like, if anyone asks you a question (unless it's George Clooney or Salma Hayek) the correct answer will always be "no."

"No, you can't have my other chair."

"No, I haven't seen the purse snatcher."

"No, I'm not interested in subscribing to any magazine on that long list of yours."

"No, I'm not anyone famous. I get that all the time."

"No, I have NO money."

"No, I won't sign that petition." (If the activist won't give up, just sign it with a made up name or use a friend's identity. It's faster than listening to his or her cause.)

The only time you should be saying "yes" is if you really want to spend four dollars on a stolen stereo. I don't advise this, although stolen equipment is often more reliable than used.

Upscale fast-food joints used to be great places to sit and chill out for hours. (Not so much lately.) Once again, it's easy to blend. The volume is pretty high, and you generally buy your food at a counter and go back to a table with it. This removes the need for a waiter or waitress to be involved in the comings and goings of your time spent there. There's nothing worse than having a waiter tap his or her feet impatiently, right next to your table.

If you do find yourself hanging out an unusually long time at a restaurant that has table service, do be careful that you're not overstaying your welcome. Again, I've been that person stalling at the table, and I've also been that waitress. All I have to say is, if you plan on loitering there for hours at a clip, then throw money at the waiter right when you sit down. This is the only way to alleviate the pressure from management. Also, pick times in between the lunch hour and the dinner rush. They can't hate you too much when they have no one waiting for a table.

There used to be a fantastic fast-food sushi restaurant near where I once lived in the West Village, called Go Sushi. It was a great place to sit and do nothing. In fact, they even encouraged people to do nothing by lining the walls with magazines, an added bonus. It was like a public library where you could eat and be loud without having to search endlessly through the racks of periodicals in order to find something current.

Not many people took advantage of that great space. Customers ate and left and I never understood why. I must have spent more time there in a day than everyone else put together.

The great thing about doing nothing and hanging out in public places is you're actually doing nothing, but you *look* like you're doing something because you are *somewhere*. You are, at the same time, however, subject to other people's energy and personal drama. You're putting yourself out there in a world where anything could happen at any time. What can begin as basic chilling sometimes becomes exciting! The element of surprise can often be a welcome intrusion. Then again, sometimes it can be a royal pain in the ass.

Sidebar: I will provide you with an example: It was one of those overcast days that most people hate, but I adore. (Nothing validates doing nothing more than a cloudy day.) I was still living in New York and hanging out in Go Sushi at the time. I was sitting at a table facing the window and eating something called a "spider roll." I wasn't exactly sure what was in it, but it was mostly fried and crunchy and tasted great.

Forgoing the chopsticks and stabbing the last few bites with a plastic fork, I grabbed the latest issue of *Cosmopolitan* and started reading up on all the feminine things I should be doing with my life. I had been under the impression that *Cosmopolitan* was geared toward top women executives who could balance a high-powered career, yet still manage to hang onto a darling husband and raise four kids. I was wrong. It is all about sex, and since I was having plenty of sex (exception to the rules), reading about it was unnecessary. I got up and switched my magazine to *People*. It's always fun to read about Jennifer Aniston's new hairstyle.

On my way back to the table, I noticed the one lecherous dude I always avoided. I admired how he took advantage of Go Sushi, such as I did, but I still hated that he was always around. In my opinion, he was the mascot snag of Go Sushi. He was persistent and always attempted to ask me the same questions. I learned early on to put on my Walkman the second I spotted him.

The first time I ran into him, he tried to corner me by the green tea and red bean ice-cream cooler. He asked me if I was the woman who wrote for a motorcycle magazine. Apparently, there is a woman out there with the same laptop as mine that writes for *Motorcycle Monthly* while she dines on chicken teriyaki. I do not look like the type who knows the first thing about motorcycles. I'm lucky I can recognize a moped when I see one.

Upon spotting him on this unlucky day, I raced back to the table and buried myself in the magazine before he could notice me. I breathed a sigh of relief and read for thirty minutes about which stars were getting liposuction. I bought another ginger ale. I traded my *People* magazine for *Maxim* and read about men's "secret desires." Hah! If they were really secret they would be deranged and, therefore, not expanded upon in this popular magazine. I read about the basic sex fantasies anyway: sex with two girls. I rolled my eyes.

At that moment, a homeless man found his way past my table begging for money. Homeless people are snags by definition, but I have a soft spot for them. I also don't like to be hassled, so I generally give them something. I recalled the idiot compassion theory I learned years before in a college psychology class. According to the "experts" giving the homeless money is not really helping them. I'm not sure I buy that, especially when handing them a cold beer lights up their face. They're usually content with money, food, or booze and we both feel happy about it. Why does that make me an idiot?

Since I actually didn't have any beer on me at that given moment, I gave this poor guy a dollar. (This was 2002 when a dollar went a little further.) I remember thinking that if he collected another dollar, he'd be able to buy his own beer. I felt I contributed to that. Ultimately, if you want to keep doing nothing, you must pay people to stay away from you. You do not need some wacko publicly belting out curse words at you. One of the words is bound to hit a nerve, and you might end up in jail rather than being out a dollar. Plus, if you can sit in a restaurant for two hours, the homeless person needs the money more than you do.

Since I'm on the topic, some homeless people are inspiring. All they do is beg and try to stay warm. They go to the extreme in order to do nothing. They aren't concerned with the Dow Jones Industrial Average. You have to remember that most of them were not always homeless. Some opted for it and others fell into their predicament. My philosophy is to avoid them and support them so they stay out of my way. End of subject.

I went back to catching up on my current affairs. Having read most of Go Sushi's literary collection, I was left with *Time* and *Parenting*. I frowned. What the fuck was I going to do with a magazine that discussed kids? And I lived in New York City. What did I need to read *Time* Magazine for? History was happening all around me. I looked out the window instead and watched the clouds outside burst into a storm. People raced around trying to avoid the downpour. It was like watching ants scurry in different directions when you pour Sprite into their anthill. Watching people get wet is fun.

By this time I was hungry again, so I bought some seaweed salad to munch on. As I was purchasing it, the guy at the table next to me started hyperventilating. He was complaining of feeling terribly dizzy and nervous all of a sudden. I quickly glanced down in front of him to make sure he wasn't eating a spider roll.

"I feel like I'm dying!" he cried out, holding his head. For some reason, an image of Woody Allen popped into my mind. Then he started screaming. "I feel so weird! Help me! Help me!"

Talk about making a scene. The cute girl with him was turning a shade of purple you rarely see. She looked worse than he did.

"What's wrong with you?" the girl demanded, obviously concerned as well as embarrassed.

"I don't know, it came on all of a sudden. The whole room is swirling in front of me!" the guy howled.

"OK . . . just calm down," the girl said, anxiously looking around.

Everyone remaining in Go Sushi was now transfixed on the couple (including the mascot snag of the establishment.)

"I don't know what's going on!" he screamed, "Somebody call 911!"

The girl's mouth dropped open.

"Do you think it was something you ate?" she asked.

"All I had was a soda!" he screamed at her. The whole room sighed with relief. Me included.

"Does anyone have a cell phone?" he cried. "Can someone please call an ambulance?"

I just stared at this young, disturbed man in disbelief. I concluded he was either having a panic attack or he was about to pull off the con of the century. I was secretly glad I left my cell phone at home.

He then promptly passed out. I watched his head fall squarely onto the middle of the table. Suspiciously, I wondered if he was performing an acting exercise. Would he jump up any second and start asking for donations toward drama classes? No one else must have considered this because four people miraculously all reached for their cell phones at the same time.

I felt bad for the girl. I beckoned her over to me. "Believe it or not, I've seen something similar to this before," I whispered. "The other dude fainted in a Häagen-Dazs store. An employee stuck an ice cream cone on the man's forehead and after a couple minutes he came to. Let's get something cold for your friend," I insisted.

The girl looked at me like I was crazy and then agreed with me, probably out of sheer discomfort. "OK, if you think it will help."

What did I know? I was certainly no doctor, but I still asked the Go Sushi employee next to me for some ice cream to shock the victim. Being the moron he was, he asked me which flavor. Whichever? I yelled. It wasn't like the red bean was colder than the green tea, for God's sake. Everyone was now peering at the three of us.

I pressed the green tea ice cream on the side of his neck, shining like Florence Nightingale during the Crimean War.

Nothing happened other than it began to melt and drip down his back.

The good news was Go Sushi was only a block away from St. Vincent's Hospital, so the ambulance came quickly. I'd rather professionals handle situations like these anyway. I backed up and watched the sticky dude get carted out on a stretcher. It was like a West Village episode of ER.

For some reason, I didn't feel like staying there much longer after that, so I did finally go home. I will never know if that guy was seriously ill, crazy, or just having a bad day. I'll never know what happened to him, or if I helped save him with the ice cream.

That's one of the small risks you take in hanging out extensively in coffee shops and restaurants. Your chances of experiencing strange things with no resolution increase dramatically. On the flip side, theatrical events can be most enjoyable in terms of adding a little excitement to your day. To recap, the advantages of doing nothing in highly populated public places far outweigh the risks. These days, however, it is not as sensible an option.

CHAPTER 11

Part 1

Causing A Scene
(How To Calm The Inner Tiger)

I'm sure that everyone at one time has witnessed an act of pure drama. We've all seen people make scenes that belong in campy, B movies. Whether people divert their eyes when a couple starts screaming at each other in public, or stop everything and start cheering when the fistfight breaks out, don't we all think the same thing? *They are totally embarrassing each other!*

You think how ridiculous they look. You think *I'd never do that.* That is why it is very important to never lose your cool. Not only is it a waste of energy – you'll look like an asshole! Unless, of course, you are doing it for sheer entertainment purposes. If privacy isn't your specialty, causing a scene is a great way to spice up doing nothing.

On a similar note, it's important to stay out of situations that have nothing to do with you. I know how hard it can be to keep your big mouth shut. Tempting as it may be, it's always best to avoid circumstances that don't concern you.

I still have difficulty with what I'm advocating, but I have learned from my mistakes.

In my younger, more naive years, I was always the type to pick a side. If Ellen was my friend and she was in a fight with Judy, then I'd be the one to curse Judy out. Two days later, Ellen and Judy were back to being buddy-buddy, and *I* was the one Judy never spoke to again. Not to mention, Ellen then became less of a friend because of my rage. At any rate, my behavior didn't help to advance my popularity. However, everyone seemed afraid of me, which is better than being popular.

By senior year in high school, ninety-five percent of my class had suffered my wrath at one time or another. I'm not sure how I had any friends at all. Now we're all close-as-could-be on Facebook.

Getting back to the point, don't create scenes. It's simply too much work. Lack of involvement equals more time for you. More time for you translates into more time doing nothing. I'm going to give you another example in a roundabout way. I wrote this segment in January of 2020, when COVID was only just beginning to be discussed in America.

Sidebar: Since I'm sitting at Starbucks again, I'll use what's happening here to justify the importance of not getting involved.

A field trip consisting of at least forty little kids has been launched and catapulted from the nearest public school – I assume by bus. At this very moment, they are all racing in. The two weary chaperones are bringing up the rear of this parade. They both look exhausted.

Starbucks seems like an odd choice for a large group of third graders, but I guess times have changed. The chaperones must have been desperate for a caffeine fix. (That's my guess.)

I feel bad for the Starbucks employees; you know every single kid will order a frozen drink. Kids under ten do not understand the true meaning of coffee yet. Or maybe they do these days. Either way, since the army of minions has invaded my office, the noise level in the room has elevated from a low library buzz to that of grade school recess. What's even more amusing is watching the typical Starbucks customer walk in, notice the line and the commotion, and walk back out. This, I enjoy. The rest . . . no. I yearn for Manhattan, where there's another Starbucks across the street. *I can't get in my car right now and drive three miles. I simply don't have the energy, and that would also constitute doing something.* Having no choice but to listen to the elevated demands for S'mores Frappuccinos, I'm finding it extremely difficult to concentrate. Every few minutes I hear a bad rendition of a high-pitched, Arnold Jackson from *Diff'rent Strokes. Whatcha talkin' bout Willis?* This has me really puzzled. I mean, how do these kids even know about that ancient show? All I can think is the reruns must be trending on YouTube.

Remember I said roundabout? Stay with me.

There are only two employees working the counter. I'm thinking one ran out to get more ice and the other two just ran out forever. I get it.

I look around and note that all the college students

are packing up their personal up-to-the-minute electronics in order to head to quieter, trendier locations. "I can't deal with kids," one murmured under his breath, receiving an empathetic glance from his friend. Heaven forbid they studied in their respective apartments. Although, in their defense, there is no room to study in what they could possibly afford at their age. I smile anyway, thinking these older kids are smart to bolt. I approve and applaud their superior attitude problems.

I turn my attention back to the counter line, thinking I might like some bacon gouda egg bites. In the midst of the chaos, one of the two employees has decided to interview someone for a job. Now! Are you kidding me? You're leaving the one poor girl alone, running from one blender to another. I feel like jumping back there and helping her, but I'm sure I'd cause some liability suit. Not to mention, I would steal all the brownies.

If I had a decent bone in my body, I'd call corporate and tell them to send backup, but that would be expending far too much energy. They'd be asking *me* if I wanted a job, and so on. I don't need that hassle. I'd have to decline, for obvious reasons. As hard as it was to look away when the counter girl knocked over all the large coffee cups, I did.

Instead, I glanced over at the moron in the Starbucks cap interviewing the pretty blond who couldn't have been older than sixteen. I felt like tapping him on the shoulder and saying, "Tell Barbie to come back when you're not flooded by a busload of kids!" I considered expressing my opinion, but I didn't want to lose my favorite table just to make another enemy. I chose not to make a scene. Case in point.

CHAPTER 11
Part 2
Trying Too Hard. Just Don't.

The more entangled and attached you get in life, the more heartbreak and disappointment. Not to throw in too many childhood references, but how often did you get stupidly excited for a school event, spend hours getting ready, only to come home extremely disappointed? *Maybe only girls did that?* Attempting to find out if this was true, I asked my boyfriend at the time – who is now my ex-husband – if he'd had similar experiences. He looked at me like I was stupid and said, "Wouldn't know – my friends and I were too busy smoking pot behind the bleachers." That information didn't prove particularly helpful to me and my quest for answers.

What I have learned is that good things only happen when you're not expecting it. If you exert any effort toward making things right or setting something up, you may as well forget it. It follows along the lines of the famous saying, "No good deed goes unpunished."

In fact, when I met my future ex-husband, I wasn't trying to make it happen. I was introduced to him when I reluctantly took a job at a restaurant where he was one of the chefs. I thought he was obnoxious and cocky, and he wore far too many concert T-shirts for my liking. Hence, I did not pursue him as a romantic conquest. The restaurant job itself was intended to be temporary. Who would have thought it was going to create a whole new and interesting life for me? A different time, a different decade, but the point is still the same: if you're not actively trying too hard, good things will find you.

Reversing the scenario, how many other times did I fall for some nut job and plan my every movement around when I would get a chance to see him again? Such as when I fell for the doorman at Mercury Lounge. I went to this particular bar three times a week, pretending I was a band aficionado despite hating live music. Nothing between the door guy and me ever transpired. Come to think of it, I never even got his name. After a month, I realized I was wasting my time and door-entry money. I also felt that if I had to listen to another new band singing original music, I would kill myself.

In addition, trying too hard with a person you meet through an obligatory function or event is never a good idea since he or she often turns out to be a snag. Merely being acquainted with someone is often best. Just because you are hobnobbing at the same gala doesn't mean you have to like the person. You don't have to pretend to be overcome with joy when they find you hiding behind a large potted plant. There is also no point in being falsely effusive or overly polite. It's tiring.

Have you ever noticed that when strangers are too afraid to ask you for your phone number, they ask if you have e-mail? What the fuck is that about? If they are instinctively smart enough to pick up on the fact that you might not feel comfortable giving your number out, then why do they think your personal e-mail is up for grabs?

Super smart advice: Only share your e-mail address if you actually think you'll return their e-mail. Otherwise, you'll just continue to exert precious energy for no reason.

Sometimes, we can get a little hyper for no particular reason. Maybe we're excited about something or woke up in a good mood for a change. Whatever the explanation may be, it can make the wrong initial impression with people we're meeting for the first time. In order to prevent being mistakenly labeled as outgoing, we should hide our upbeat mood (sometimes labeled as mania) from strangers. This means not being overly friendly when we don't know what the other person is thinking. If the person is cool, they'll automatically think we're trying too hard. If they're weirdos, they'll assume we're attracted to them. Either way, you look stupid.

Under this demonic influence of high energy – further enhanced by lack of sleep, too much caffeine, hard liquor, odd herbs, cold medicines, or speed – we can possibly become our own worst enemy. When we relax and regain our senses, we're sometimes faced with upcoming plans or arrangements that we suggested, but no longer wish to keep. We must detect when this bizarre mood is coming on, then tone it down before it gets out of hand. Prevention is key. Blow out the match before the fire starts.

When you receive invites, keep your cool and have your excuses at the ready. *I think I have something to do that day. I'll check my calendar and get back to you*, is a perfect response.

If you hear yourself making plans with people you don't

know yet – stop yourself. It's almost like applying sunblock before you get burned. It will be less painful later.

CHAPTER 12

Living With A Significant Other
And Keeping On The Path

I know what you're thinking. How on earth did I ever manage to hold onto one guy? Well, I didn't actually, but who's counting? What I'm about to tell you is good news, so don't panic.

Begin by eradicating from your memory all those myths about how much work relationships take. The true definition of work is doing something you don't necessarily want to do for an extended period of time. If you are living with a significant other, or you are married, that should be something you have chosen. *Ideally.* Hence, it is not something to be looked upon as work, no matter how difficult getting along may seem at times.

When you wake up and your partner is snuggled between your elbow and hip bone and you can't feel the right side of your body, it gives you a sense of intimacy at best. Who else would allow this? De-pretzelizing yourself in order to regain your natural circulation can be a lovely start to your day. Chances are, your companion will wake up when you shove him or her off you, and soon you may even be taking part in the first exception to the rule: having sex! Ta-Da!

Since my current husband, Ron, would be less than pleased if I discussed our bedroom life in a non-fiction book, I'm going to rewind to 2003, and use my ex-husband as an example in this chapter. I know he won't care.

Many days I awoke to find myself completely uncovered with no blanket in sight. I'd look over and see Vince sleeping soundly under the covers with one arm thrown over his head and his mouth wide open. I often thought it would be a perfect time to take a throat culture. When he was in this position, he was usually making a slight gasping noise like each breath might be his last. When he was snoring, which wasn't often, thank God, I would pinch his nose until he couldn't breathe. I always got a kick out of his reaction. He'd wake up with a fright, knowing I was up to my old tricks.

You would think that living with someone and sharing your life might interfere with your "nothing" priorities, but surprisingly, it really doesn't. The experiences you share with others never have to be things you don't want to do, or feel strange about, as long as you're living with the right person, during the right time in your life. If you have to hide information about yourself and act interested in shit you could care less about, then not only are you doing too much, you're doing something wrong!

For instance, if my current husband is going on and on about something I could care less about, I don't pretend to be interested. I just tune him out. The other day he suggested I should get my ears checked, and maybe I will, but there is nothing wrong with my hearing!

The same can be applied to other relationships, whether

it's a close friend or your mother. If you don't particularly care what he or she is talking about, just don't listen. Look into their eyes while they speak, study their facial features, and block them out. They will never accuse you of interrupting them.

Naturally, living with another human being can pose a challenge when your focus is on doing as little as possible. My advice is to let your partner know what your priorities are right at the beginning of the relationship. This way there will be no confusion. Eventually your companion will get to know the real you anyway. Whether he or she likes it or not. It's just as well they know what you're all about from the start so they're not startled or envious by your stress-free, uncomplicated life. I know that worked for me. Over my lifetime, I can honestly say I did my partners a huge favor; they always knew what to expect.

Under my school of thought, using me as an example, every conversation should be like this one:

Him: *"What did you do today?"*
Her: *"Not much. I had a great day."*
Him: *"Of course, you did."*

This leads to fewer arguments in the long run. Please be aware that the same concepts do not apply for everyone. If you're unemployed and not pulling your weight, hanging out all day at the park, beach, newsstand or bar, you'd better have some great lies ready on the tip of your tongue. I agree that everyone should do nothing, but some information should be kept to yourself in order to continue to do less.

When remaining on the path of nothingness, it is important not to let your significant other persuade you into doing things for the sake of it, or doing things just because they would like you to. I'll give you an example. Again, taken from over a decade ago:

Sidebar: I don't cook. Before 2020, I hadn't cooked a thing since that ridiculous class final (refer back to Chapter 7 if you must). I did, however, access my local deli and pick up minor items such as cheese, soda, and the occasional carton of milk. Picking up items at the deli was part of my routine. You could almost call it a systematic way of ensuring I didn't starve to death. I'm going to use Vince again since he's so easy to make fun of.

He and I were having a mundane discussion about how I "blow money." His words, not mine.

I recall rolling my eyes and mocking him. "Tell me how I squander my earnings. Please enlighten me with an example of my foolish antics, darling." I cracked my knuckles and yawned.

"No, forget it, you're just going to make fun of me," he growled, shifting away from me on the sofa.

I had to pretend to be serious for a minute. "No, really, tell me. It might be useful. You never know . . ." I tried to keep a straight face.

"Well, for starters you have no regard for prices. You just buy stuff whenever and wherever you feel like it."

"Are you accusing me of not being a comparative shopper?" I furrowed my brows in an effort to look sincere.

"Compare? You don't even know the price of something to compare it."

What he was saying was true, but it wasn't like the difference of five cents on a nectarine was ever going to matter to me. "Dude, come on. You don't see me lounging around in Prada and sleeping in Christian Dior. Buying a fancy car and shit."

"First of all, you don't know how to drive. Secondly, I'm not talking about that. I'm talking about the little stuff that adds up. You might buy six Cokes from the deli in one day when you could have gotten a six-pack at the supermarket for like, half the price."

I stared at him. Then I burst out laughing.

"OK, I'm glad I amuse you. Forget it!" he said angrily.

"Do we live near any supermarkets?" I was dead serious.

"There's actually one two blocks north of us on west side of Sixth Avenue."

"It's not registering. What's it called?"

"It's a Food Emporium," he said, looking very smug.

"Oh yeah, I have seen it. It keeps similar hours to the bank. It's closed by the time I walk to work. Very convenient." I yawned again.

"It's twenty-four hours, Amy."

"Not unless you have your own key," I scoffed. I couldn't *believe* we were having this conversation.

"OK, whatever," he said, "You're obviously not going to change, so never mind."

For some reason that comment irritated me. "Who

gives a shit about the price of mixed nuts? Furthermore, you better hope I never step foot in a supermarket to save three cents because I'll wind up spending another fifty bucks on stuff that I think looks fun! Like a new cereal by Nabisco, or a new strain of fruit. Not to mention, if I venture into the candy aisle, you can say goodbye to your counter space."

"Amy – "

"Plus, at the deli you're paying the extra ten cents for the effort your saving. I don't have to maneuver myself through ten aisles of crap to find the frigging trash bags. That's worth a dollar right there! It's like people paying for a bus to take them to Key Food in Riverdale to save a total of five bucks. It makes no sense."

I would have continued, but he rudely interrupted me. "Enough! Forget I said anything, just carry on. But stop complaining about having no money."

The discussion moved onto other points of contention at the time, but my argument should be clear. Just because my ex liked to buy his economy bag of Ruffles at a supermarket between the hours of eleven and four didn't mean I had to run to Gristedes every time I needed a Coke to mix with my rum.

Now when living with a significant other and remaining on the path of nothingness, always be sure to reinforce your point. A couple days after the discussion with Vince over my multiple trips to the deli, I told him a little story. The story went like this:

"Earlier today I was picking up a couple of things

at the deli. It was wicked cold so I had on that stupid orange hat that glows in the dark – you know the one. Anyway, I put my Snickers bar and my caffeine-free Coke on the counter. During that time, a man behind me set down a carton of orange juice and two oranges. I thought that was cute so I said, 'Felt like some orange?' but I didn't look at the person buying it. I was rummaging through my pockets for cash at the time.

'Your hat inspired me,' this guy said, in a deep, familiar voice.

I glanced up, remembering my stupid hat, and saw that I was talking to Sean Connery. Of all days to be looking like I was directing traffic, I couldn't believe it. I grabbed my change and ran out the door. I felt like such a dick."

Vince was already chuckling, but I wasn't done yet. "I raced out of there, but what I should have done was tell him it would have been cheaper if he shopped at the supermarket. He could have saved a dollar!"

Vince stopped laughing. It was very satisfying. Justifying your original argument with humorous anecdotes is a great way to reiterate your initial argument.

Another tactic that works rather well, even though I don't truly agree with it, is placating the person you live with on a subject of which you don't see eye to eye. As it is usually my last resort, I try to save it for the really tough issues on which I'll never in my lifetime agree.

However, if it's at the end of a long day and you don't feel like arguing, by all means, just tell your significant other,

"Yes, you're right. That's what I'll do from now on. You got it."

When the issue comes up again, do whatever you bloody well please. Say you changed your mind – whatever. It's amazing how the same issues will keep coming up over and over again until they're resolved. Remain strong and secure enough to know what you want and stand by your decisions. Keep in mind that your loved ones should be standing by you as you continue your crusade of doing less and enjoying life more.

Also remind yourself that you don't have to do absolutely everything together. For instance, if he or she wants to take a karate class once a week, you don't have to suddenly act like you love martial arts. If his dream vacation consists of climbing Mt. Everest in December, it doesn't mean you can't relax in the Bahamas while you wait for him to get it out of his system. (See next chapter on vacationing.)

Plus, couples that like all the same things get bored with each other. I think that's why so many musician and actor couples break up. It's always better to be different. I think if I was actually one of those people that cut out coupons and shopped wisely, Vince and I wouldn't have stayed married as long as we did.

Opposites do attract; the saying is true. I think that's because each of us always wishes we were a little more like the other person. That's why the boring science teacher always falls for the wild stripper and vice versa. (I suggest renting *Weird Science* starring Kelly LeBrock for anyone who doesn't believe me.)

The only things you both must enjoy, of course, are the four exceptions to the rules: having sex being the most important. This is a given.

To sum up quickly, living with another can enrich your life in many aspects. As long as you stay your own person, you should not be at risk for losing your identity or your mind. If your partner respects you, he or she will support you in your goals, however different they may be from his or her own. Loving someone entails loving everything about them, or at least accepting their quirks. Trust me, once your partner experiences the carefree nothing you embody, your magic will inspire them to be more like you.

CHAPTER 13

Part 1

Vacationing: A True Art Form

I was not prepared for a global pandemic when I began writing this book. Therefore, try to remember better days when we longed for a vacation without today's restrictions and health risks.

Because vacationing is all about doing nothing!

"I need a vacation!" should be the national motto for our country. Forget all that "with liberty and justice for all." *Just book me on the next flight to anywhere other than here.* And do it quickly!

Taking a vacation, not a trip, (I'll go over the differences in the second part of this chapter), is the perfect escape from your routine existence. According to my gospel, vacationing paves the road to becoming a perfect soul. If you associate vacationing with laziness, get over it. Forget any negative references to idleness you may have overheard or been lectured on growing up. Think back to the people who chastised you for being uninspired and inactive and think of what miserable lives they led. Most parents would be a perfect example. They simply did not understand that our sole purpose was to have fun on this merry-go-round we call life.

The definition of "vacation," according to the Webster's dictionary, is "a scheduled period during which activity is suspended." Now, if we don't do much on a daily basis, there's really not that much of a distinction between everyday life and vacation time, is there? Hah! We'd like to think so. Unfortunately, unwelcome surprises can always pop up in our natural habitats. For example, an old pipe could break and flood your whole apartment. If you were on vacation, you wouldn't even know it. This is why I recommend switching up the scenery as often as possible.

Each individual has a different view of a dream vacation. Some people think that touring the Egyptian pyramids for three weeks would be fun. I do not. Sunbathing by a nice pool, sipping a frozen drink off the Bermuda coastline is more my speed. However, resting by a pool in Florida or South Carolina during high season might suffice. To be honest, I probably wouldn't know the difference.

The important thing to come away with is to treat life as a permanent vacation. If an opportunity arises to vacation in another location, there are a few I recommend, and a few I suggest you avoid. These are my top five recommendations.

◆ All Tropical Islands Within a Five-Hour Flying
 Distance

For anyone uncertain about the meaning of tropical, this does not include Long Island. If you live on the East Coast, the Virgin Islands, Bermuda, and the Caribbean are my top three picks. Forget Hawaii. The extra ten hours in the sky detract from its allure. Those who live on the West Coast can enjoy this little treasure.

Islands offer little to do, tons of outdoor relaxing, plenty of tropical cocktails, good tanning weather, sultry storms and beautiful accommodations. (Avoid hurricane season.) The islands provide romantic settings if you go with a loved one and a relatively active singles scene if you're single. Entertainment and nightlife is usually just one step away. Islands also tend to offer rather good values on air travel and lodging. Whatever supplies you might need are affordable, bordering on cheap.

♦ France or Italy Pre-2020

These countries aren't called wine regions for nothing. As long as you forgo the sightseeing and bring lots of money, these two countries offer numerous cafés where you can drink wine and eat cheese all day long. The natives encourage smoking and drinking. In fact, some places even discourage nonsmoking and refuse to sell soft drinks or give out water. Ha! To think I had nothing to do with setting these fine guidelines! This vacation, of course, doesn't include the Eiffel Tower and the Leaning Tower of Pisa. Tall buildings are indicative of stairs.

Paris is a very romantic city, so the rumor goes. I've never been, but from what I've seen on TV, most of the buildings look dirty and old. In addition, one of my aunts got divorced shortly after returning from a trip to Paris. My uncle met someone he liked better over there. Unfortunately for my aunt, it was only mood enhancing for Uncle Jim.

♦ Spas and Resorts

Talk about a vacation within a vacation! However, be alert when picking a particular spa, as sometimes there is confusion between a spa-resort and a wellness camp. I'll explain the difference and how to prevent making a huge mistake.

Spas and resorts offer *luxury pampering.* They are usually quite expensive, and provide services such as aromatherapy massage, Swedish massage, assorted hydrotherapy body treatments, nail and hair care, and facials. Reflexology, mud wraps, and acupuncture are available for the more daring.

Resorts primarily focus on leisurely activities. Allow me to remind you, everything a spa has to offer is provided for YOU. You do nothing except admire the people assisting you in becoming a beautiful, relaxed creature.

Eating gourmet food and drinking excellent wine is all part of the exquisite spa experience. There are some wonderful spas in the Southwest that are definitely worth the trip, such as JW Marriott Scottsdale Camelback Inn Resort & Spa in Arizona. The spa concentrates on providing the opportunity to rest and rejuvenate while experiencing their latest New Age treatments. The resort even offers what they call a "Parisian body polish," which utilizes crushed pearls to make your skin smooth and silky. That's definitely something I wouldn't try at home alone. Would you?

Notice I have only used an example in the United States. Why go across the pond when it's all in your backyard?

Wellness camps are another story altogether. Any place that concentrates more on sports conditioning, health, medical wellness, or strict nutrition and diet are places to be avoided. These places fall under the headline of camps, which I expand on later in this chapter.

♦ College Party Towns

Highly recommend! There's really not so much to say about these towns except for the obvious. Even if you know absolutely no one, you will make friends in an instant by walking into a local bar. In the early fall and late spring, try Amherst, Massachusetts. People party in their Patagonia, and you don't have to enroll in the university to fit in. Just grab a red plastic cup and join in the party like you are old alumni. Other great collegiate options include Portland, Maine; Cambridge, Massachusetts; Morgantown, West Virginia and Austin, Texas.

If you want warm, try Tempe, Arizona, the home of Arizona State University and see if you can keep up with the drinkers they breed down near the desert. Another bonus is I've never seen a single person studying in these towns; I only see them taking part in the four exceptions to the rules: having sex, drinking, eating, and smoking. In fact, between five and fifteen percent of the student population flunk out each year due to these inspiring environments. School or no school, these towns seem to encourage doing nothing!

♦ Beaches

Even though I'm not particularly fond of the ocean – as it is glaring proof of the lack of control we have over our lives – I still recommend the beach for quick getaways. A couple days relaxing in Naples, Florida, can make all the difference. On the East Coast of Florida, I suggest Jupiter as opposed to Miami. (Although South Beach used to be a kick-ass good time. Nikki Beach Club being my hands down favorite.)

Beach areas give way to an active bar scene with easygoing vibes.

Have you ever noticed a beach town can really improve a dreary state? Take Rhode Island for example. Rhode Island would be a wash if it weren't for Newport Beach and Narragansett. Massachusetts would be less enticing without Nantucket and the Berkshires. (Cape Cod is overrated.) And what redeeming quality does Delaware have besides its strip of beaches starting with Rehoboth and ending with Bethany? Don't tell me Dover Air Force Base gets your juices flowing. I could go on and on, heading south down the country, but I've already effectively proven my point.

And I'm not even talking about the beautiful beaches of the world here because they are simply too far away. Hence, I've never been. I'm sure the isles of Greece are kinky paradises and the Brazilian beaches produce fresh, perfect coconuts.

I have made one solid conclusion about which vacation incorporates all the desirable things about doing nothing in style if you decide to ignore my five-hour flying limit: Sardinia, Italy! White sand beaches! Sunsets! Good wine! Nightlife! Sunbathing on boats!

Come to think of it, who cares about a college town?

CHAPTER 13

Part 2

Avoid Trips At All Times

After discussing vacations, I really hate to talk about this nasty four-letter word. The opposite of a vacation is a trip. A trip is a horrendous experience that is usually supported by reasoning – another enemy that works against us doing nothing. If you work for a company, and they send you away on business, that's why it's called a business trip. You have to work. Business trips revolve around schedules, and in most cases your schedule will be taken up with conferences, meetings, and conventions on boring subjects like air preservation and tax auditing.

But not all trips are business related. Sometimes there is confusion between what we label a trip for some and a vacation for others. I'm going to be very clear when I list trips now. Here are the top six worst trips you can inflict on yourself and whomever has fooled you into joining them.

♦ Educational Experience Trips

Who cares? An experience that revolves around learning is rarely fun. Similar to a "business trip," it doesn't matter how old you are, these trips lack excitement. Remember being dragged to Epcot Center when you were nine – dying instead to see Mickey Mouse ten feet away? If your parents couldn't afford Epcot, trust me, you were better off. MGM Studios was all hype too. Seeing the studios at MGM at a young age was like being lost among a bunch of machinery and trying to relate it to an actual movie.

Destinations like this still exist. I compare it to the theme restaurant that just won't go away. Half of which I've had the misfortune of working at during one desperate point or another. Did you know that Space Aliens Grill & Bar just opened a third location?

Just for the record, I will admit that Florida improved Epcot Center. I actually went again about three years ago. Now there is a section for adults, and learning about other countries is actually fun – with the addition of cocktails! Cute bars and restaurants represent specific countries. I'm not up to date on how many countries we have now, but Epcot Center opened a significant number of party spots. You can drink a Scottish Ale in "Scotland," slug a pint of Guinness in "Ireland," or slam a shot of Don Julio Tequila in "Mexico."

♦ Cruises

I have always loathed the idea of being on a ship sailing across the rocky sea with other families comprised of snags. I successfully avoided it up until five years ago. It just seemed like a really stupid idea. Now I can confirm that it was.

I went on this three-day weekend cruise because I was brainwashed and coerced by those closest to me. I will not mention any names, as you know who you are. To make a long story short, I hated almost every minute of it, and I will NEVER do it again.

Reasons why:

- It throws off your equilibrium, leading to instant dizziness.
- The food sucks.
- I wouldn't wish that carpeting on my worst enemy.
- You're always climbing stairs to get from one section of the ship to another.
- On big boats, you are always lost, which leads to more stairs.
- No one tells you how noisy ships are. I'm here to tell you they are loud as hell.
- Most cruise lines are limited to cheap liquor.
- Apart from a river cruise, you rarely see land – where's the security in that?

If you need further convincing, watch one of these movies: *Death Ship* (1980); *The Perfect Storm* (2000) or *Ghost Ship* (2002). Given the box office success of *Titanic*, I'm not going to insult my readers' intelligence. Everyone has seen this movie.

♦ Wellness Camps

This is the absolute worst trip you can agree to. It is not

to be referred to as a spa or resort at any point of reference. Any place in the woods that keeps you on a time schedule beginning extremely early in the morning and continuing into the evening is not a vacation. Join the army. Whether it's a spiritual camp, a rigorous fitness camp, or an educational camp, it amounts to the same thing: the exchange of your hard-robbed money in return for guidance through slow, torturous activities, one after the other, in the spirit of self-improvement.

Don't let anyone talk you into going. I'm serious now. It's bad. Opt instead for a vacation. My mother once convinced me that I would enjoy a week of glorified camp located in upstate New York. (I'd love to announce the name, but it's better I don't because some people might actually like it and be offended.) Let's just say it was holistic. I will provide a one-day example of my pain.

6 a.m. Breakfast. A wheat-free, vegan breakfast of dry oats and soy milk. (Back when soy wasn't frowned upon.) I was barely awake so I don't remember if I tried to eat it or not.

7 a.m. Yoga. I just tried to touch my toes and laughed at my mother who thought she was keeping up with the rest of the class.

8 a.m. Some fucking lecture on a subject that might have been meditation. So enlightened in my foreign, catatonic state, I instantly fell back asleep until the class bell woke me up at ten a.m., three days in a row.

I was then lurched into the following acts of unkindness:

10:15 a.m. African soul dance movement. You can imagine how graceful I appeared with no rhythm bouncing around in my Nikes.

11:25 a.m. Sermon on the Buddhist religion.

12:30 p.m. Lunch. The menu was comprised of something like this: organic lentil soup, tofu fried in more soybean oil served over steamed sodium-free collard greens and three ounces of sugar-free peach "cobbler" with dairy-free whipped cream. I'm seriously not kidding. I watched my mother fake enthusiasm while I chomped down three bags of Peanut M&Ms.

1:15 p.m. Meeting with the spirituality counselor assigned to your particular cabin. This was intended to be a cathartic experience, a time for confessions. Well, I knew enough at sixteen not to admit a goddamn thing, so "Judy" talked to a brick wall for three straight afternoons.

2:30 p.m. Group counseling on topics such as addiction, mental insecurities, and health issues. They provided slides for our added enjoyment. I had to check the brochure to make sure my mother didn't sign me up for some sort type of involuntary rehab.

4 p.m. Lecture on fighting the war on corporations. At the time, I was even less political than I am now, so I wasn't aware there was a war. Hence, this was by far the most interesting part of my day. According to the teachers at this camp, corporations like Pfizer and AstraZeneca are enemies, hiding secret cures for disease. Even if this were true, I'm not sure what I could have done about it.

5 p.m. Social hour in the cafeteria. Really? I felt I was being social enough just getting along with my mother. Studying her eating cold oats at breakfast was my social hour – and wicked entertaining when I could keep my eyes open. Instead of making polite conversation with strangers who were actually enjoying this torture, I walked to the store to buy beer at five o'clock every day. Drinking was prohibited on the grounds – of course it was – but I felt my cabin was surely excluded from the rules I didn't give a shit about.

6 p.m. Dinner. Similar to lunch. I enjoyed a liquid supper in my cabin that consisted of six cans of Coors Light. My mother scolded me for refusing to detoxify the poisons in the "spiritual" environment. She was more preoccupied about me cleansing my soul than the fact I was able to acquire beer at sixteen.

7 p.m. Optional group games in the Amphitheater? "Optional" being the key word. I guzzled beer until I passed out.

While I changed the rules of the "holistic camp" to make it bearable, I would have been far happier spending my mother's money chilling in St. Croix. I think my mother agreed with me even though she wouldn't admit it, because we didn't go back again until years later when the institution offered an all-day, out-of-body experiences workshop. At that point,

I was twenty-one and my mother was fifty, and we knew to smuggle in our own food. That was a relatively interesting "trip" ending with us practicing the removal of our spirit over several bottles of wine at a bar off the Taconic Parkway.

Sidebar: I might add that when I found out about other holistic camps in the United States, I felt fortunate that there was a deli located near the camp my mother and I attended. Worse places do exist.

If anyone ever asks you to go with him or her to the Antelope Retreat and Education Center in Wyoming, just say no. Apparently, this isolated ranch puts you to work preparing meals, participating in ranch chores, and gardening. You even get to assist with herding a group of sheep to pasture in case you ever wondered how a shepherd felt on the Isle of Crete.

Wait, it gets better. According to what I've read, your shelter from Wyoming's howling gale is a tunnel built inside an earthen mound. The swimming area consists of a small stream next to a sweat lodge and rodeos are the only nearby attractions. If you don't feel like killing yourself yet, they offer a three-day wilderness fast for the truly suicidal. That might actually be better than eating the food they provide. Just guessing.

In 2002, you could participate in all this for the low rate of a hundred and fifty dollars a day, and I'm not sure that included lodging. If it still exists, I'm guessing it's double or triple the price now. I didn't think there was anything worse than camping until some nut told me about this place.

Amy Minty

♦ Climbing Mountains and Hiking Trips

I'd take working all my sorry-ass jobs over hiking three days through the woods with a thirty-pound backpack. The higher the mountain, the more dangerous the climb. If I want to risk my life, I'd rather be doing it in a lower altitude with bottle service, club music, and a bunch of my baller friends!

♦ Sleeping Outside (bad idea . . . see above)

Let's state this for the record: Passing out on your back porch or backyard does not fall under the category of a trip. You must leave your property to take a trip. In my book, however, your neighbors' backyard does indeed count. But since we're speaking frankly, the act of pioneering through the wilderness has us exerting way too much effort for absolutely no potential gain.

I actually know this for a fact because I was raised in New England by parents that actually loved camping so much, they purchased a camper. (My mother was clearly humoring my father, but she was pretty convincing.) Much to my early chagrin, I experienced this deranged kind of trip frequently. Hence, I learned early on what a mistake it is.

When you go on a camping trip, it's like signaling the sky god to rain and flood the campsite you're heading toward. Furthermore, I don't see what's fun about hanging out in the dirt, swatting mosquitoes, being miles away from any civilization, and having to cook for yourself over a bunch of burning twigs. I just don't get it. Especially when we pay good money to live under a roof. Why leave it to perch in an area of land, usually placed a half mile from the nearest communal shower? I could really get into the nitty-gritty on the subject of camping, but I don't want to come off too bitter. For bitterness, see the next excerpt on safaris.

♦ Safaris and National Reserve Parks

I don't think I was the only kid to be dragged through one of those theme park animal prisons for the day, but I think I am one of the few to unwillingly venture on a four-day safari into the heart of Zimbabwe where animals roam freely. FYI, some of the most ferocious beasts on the planet are still classified as animals.

Sidebar #2: In the summer of 1988, my mother decided to take my sister and me to Africa for the month of August. For those of you who don't know this, Zimbabwe, formally called Rhodesia under earlier British rule, was still struggling to figure out their independence. The natives did this in the form of rioting with violence and weapons. Even though I was fourteen and knew virtually nothing about other countries – still don't – I was scared shitless.

Yes, my mother still thought this trip was a good idea.

On this trip, Sarah Minty also thought a five-day camping trip was a good idea. First of all, I've made it clear how I feel about camping, so let's just picture the extreme in our minds for a moment. How do you choose between a hot, four-foot trailer that smells and a brutally cold tent that allows poisonous spiders, snakes, and insects to grab a little shelter? Which one would you prefer? Those were my two options when it came to catching a little shut-eye.

I wish that had been the worst thing about this trip. The daytime hours were like living inside a zoo. A rhinoceros would stroll past our campsite with a menacing look on his face and, unfortunately, I wasn't sure he could register mine. Furthermore, I couldn't appreciate this "once-in-a-lifetime" experience. I didn't work for *National Geographic*. I refused to take photos. I explained to my mother in great detail that I wanted no memories of the trip upon my arrival back in the states.

Who wants to remember toilets that were holes in the sand? Air misted with bugs.

Since our visit to Africa occurred in August, I assumed the weather would be hot. This is the problem with growing up in the northeast. It's also a clear example of how often I went to school, as I hadn't been taught it was winter in Africa. Still it was totally annoying that no one, including my mother, had the common decency to tell me the season. Especially when she saw me packing only shorts, T-shirts and a bathing suit. (I had no idea swimming was going to be out of the question unless I wanted to contract Bilharzia or tango with the hippos.) The lack of clothing meant I needed more bug spray than the entire camp put together.

Don't worry. It gets better. The food my mother packed was atrocious and my supply of candy ran out after the first day. There are no 7-Elevens when you're camping in the most dangerous safari in Africa. The name of the safari was Mana Pools, and the nut bags running the establishment didn't care about release forms. If a tiger ate you, too bad.

Consequently, I ate stale bread and jam for four days. Luckily, I realized I shouldn't munch on the cute, round berries I thought looked so red and juicy. Thank goodness for small favors. I'd learned inhaling buckets of bug spray wouldn't kill me, but instinctively I knew those red berries might.

What was further irritating was the sprawling campground which attempted to impose rules on us in the form of huge signs listing suggestions on how not to die on their land. For instance, we were not allowed to light a campfire unless we wanted a ring of elephants circling our campsite. Keep in mind, these were not baby elephants you see curling their trunk around nuts in a peanut butter commercial. These elephants were the size of trailers you see in more affluent motor home parks.

Another rule: we couldn't get near the Zambezi River unless we wanted to contract a deadly disease. The aforementioned Bilharzia and such. We still, however, had to rescue our drinking water from an attached canal. Or was it a stream? Who fucking knows? We still had to do this without letting the water contact our skin. It had to be boiled before drinking. That was my chore. I wore plastic gloves that almost reached my shoulders. If it had been just the boiling, I probably could have handled that, but the actually fetching of the water was something I feared. Reaching precariously over the water's edge and dipping a large saucepan into the murky gray water, concerned about a crocodile spotting my bright yellow T-shirt, was not cool. Thanks, Sarah Minty! I guess she thought it would build character, and it most certainly did.

My "chore" (English parents love and utilize this word) was still better than my sister's, if you can believe this. She was in charge of raking the leaves out of our campsite, and the leaves housed large lizards that would jump up and scare the fucking shit out of her every hour on the hour. She was twelve and probably handled it better than I would today.

Collecting, boiling, and cooling the drinking water soaked up about three hours of my day, and the rest was spent fighting with my mother's best friend's family, the same friends who had convinced my mother this would be a great "vacation" for all of us. I walked around singing America's national anthem to anyone who would listen to me.

On the third day of this magnificent mistake on my mother's part, I was standing under an enormous tree, and a snake fell on my head. That was it! I screamed so loud, I alerted every animal in a two-mile radius. Then I decided to run away. I was done.

Unfortunately, good intentions aside, I stumbled across a map of the park and saw it spread ten miles in each direction, which according to me was pretty fucking far, and I had no water or food. Or plan. Or passport, which was back in Harare. Moreover, I knew walking ten miles to a highway would increase my chances of being devoured by a lion, so I decided the campsite was a small notch above being eaten alive.

I returned three hours later, exhausted and starving, and no one had even noticed I'd been gone. It was probably because I wasn't talking to anyone after the second day. The last day I sucked it up, collected the water, boiled it, angrily distributed it, swatted bugs, and tried not to get killed by wild game.

CHAPTER 14

The Importance Of Sleep To Ensure A Relaxed Soul

Our primary goal should be to sleep as much as possible. I propose a range between eight and ten hours per night. If we can't get that much sleep, we should strive to get at least that much rest. Rest, in my definition, is lying down in an attempt to sleep.

My mother, the self-proclaimed expert on everything, says that one hour of rest is equivalent to half an hour of sleep. I'm unsure where she came up with that ratio, but I think she might be correct. With this equation in mind, meditation would also be considered half as good as sleep, as long as you are parallel with the floor.

I love sleeping once I get rolling. Sometimes I plunge headfirst into nightmares of waiting tables, but most of the time I find myself in the mall of my dreams, buying designer clothes and looking fantastic! Waking up and accepting the reality can sometimes be very disappointing.

Don't get me wrong; I often have trouble falling asleep and staying asleep. I force myself to think tired thoughts and concentrate on my breathing. I attempt to dismiss all the weird images and visions that pop into my head the moment I close my eyes. Knowing my luck, the faces I see are probably dead people trying to communicate with me. If I were a ghost, I'd be curious about me too, so I can't rule out this possibility.

No matter how hard it may be to fall asleep, we still need to get as much rest as possible. After all, sleeping and rest are the epitome of "doing nothing."

I'm a prime example of Dr. Jekyll and Ms. Hyde depending on the amount of sleep I get. Well rested, Dr. Jekyll is pleasant and carefree, dodging errands and chores with a keen sense of superiority. She avoids work at all costs. Nothing discourages or derails her in her quest for fun! She answers tricky questions brilliantly, beaming with self-confidence, an excuse at the ready. Dr. Jekyll is assertive in her quest to do as little as possible.

Ms. Hyde, on the other hand, is a completely different animal. Unable to keep a single thought straight in her head for longer than a second, Ms. Hyde spends at least forty-five minutes looking for her keys in the morning while slamming her knees into countless items of furniture. She can't remember what she's supposed to be doing, so she finds it difficult to talk her way out of any obligatory duties. Overwhelmed and easily distracted, sometimes Ms. Hyde even performs a task twice, the ultimate exasperating behavior! She forces herself through the day, unable to defend herself from the snags lurking in the distance.

Sidebar: I was Ms. Hyde not too long ago. It took me twenty minutes just to remember who I was upon waking. I rubbed the leftover makeup out of my eyes wondering why my alarm was going off. It was clearly nothing pressing, as I still haven't remembered, and this was months ago.

However that morning, I proceeded to wander aimlessly around the house. I made a latte, sat on the couch, and gave up. I remembered back to a morning in 2005. At the time, I was living in Astoria, Queens, and I had stupidly agreed to a job interview early on a Sunday morning. Naturally, after Saturday night's festivities, I had awakened in the worst version of Ms. Hyde to date.

Back in those days, I used to drop off my laundry at a laundromat five blocks away, and paid for someone else to do it. So, when I couldn't find any clean underwear, I knew where it all was.

That awful morning, I put on some of Vince's (my then husband) concert wears and walked in a semitrance down five flights of stairs to fetch my clean clothes. In my tired state, I failed to realize it was pouring rain until I was directly beneath it. I then ran to the laundromat, narrowly missing a collision with other pedestrians. Upon arrival, I stopped and glared at the black iron gate that hung down over its door. It was closed. Sunday. Were it not for the lack of sleep, I knew I wouldn't have forgotten that important detail.

On my way back to my apartment, I couldn't find my keys. I locked the door with my keys on my way out, so where the fuck were they? I did, however, find a large hole in the left pocket of Vince's ridiculous shorts. I spun around. I was not going to retrace my steps in the pouring rain.

That particular day, Vince had been at work out on Long Island, cooking brunch for four hours by the time I'd dragged myself out of bed, so I knew I'd have to locate my superintendent. Normally, Bruno was easy to find because he always stood in front of my building trying to talk to anyone who would listen. However, it being Sunday, I feared his wife might have dragged him to church, so I was relieved to see Bruno trimming the one hedge outside the building. To be fair, this hedge was his pride and joy; he clipped it twice a week, even in the rain and in the winter when it didn't grow. He was a sight to behold: a massive Yugoslavian man with dark features and thick unruly eyebrows. Whenever we stood too close, I had an urge to reach for my tweezers. He was good looking if you liked the dangerous type.

Bruno was jamming to music on his oversized, silver headphones. They looked like the kind of contraption you'd find Christopher Lloyd wearing in *Back to the Future*. It pained me to disturb Bruno. I liked him quiet. Not to mention, he was holding the largest set of gardening shears known to man.

Naturally, he was enthralled I needed his assistance. He always liked to discuss the latest movies with me that he'd watched on what he referred to as "tiny records." The DVD player had been a Christmas gift from his wife. I knew I was in for the latest broadcast.

I braced myself.

"Hey," he said, ripping off the headphones. "Did you see the new Julia Roberts movie? Mexico? Oh my." He pounded his chest. "Amazing."

"*The Mexican*, Bruno? It's not new. It came out a few years ago."

"Yeah, that one. You should really see it. That Julia. She's really something." He tapped his large fingers rapidly on his heart. "I think maybe I love her."

"Right. Listen, I locked myself out. Can you let me in with your copy?"

"What?" There was a small language barrier, which seemed to only affect me since I understood everything he said with no problem.

"I'm locked out!" I repeated with more urgency. I was being harsh, but I couldn't help it. Despite being quite dashing in a young Marlon Brando *On the Waterfront* way, Bruno was the snag of the entire block.

"You need an umbrella," he said, like that would change my situation. I stared at his eyebrows and he scowled at my wet hair.

"Yeah, well the sooner you get my key, the sooner I'll be dry, right?"

"Did you find another job yet?" he asked, clearly enjoying spending time with me.

"Bruno, please . . ."

He finally fetched the key and let me into my apartment. I was still Ms. Hyde and tired as fuck, but now irritation and annoyance surpassed my mere exhaustion. I plunked down on my couch, trying not to slouch. Bad posture is not attractive. (Sarah Minty still reminds me of this daily, despite the Atlantic Ocean between us.)

Back in my apartment in Astoria, I realized I still had no clean underwear. I put on a pair of Vince's tighty-whities – annoyed that they fit so snugly – and managed to find an outfit I truly hated, but kept around because of its high price tag. I hoped to sell it one day on eBay. Tucking the tag neatly inside the collar, I assessed my appearance in the hall mirror. Unfortunately, the outfit combined with bad lighting made me look more like a high school principal than a sexy cosmopolitan woman of the world. I knew it was all wrong, especially for a cocktail waitress job, but Ms. Hyde couldn't dredge up the energy to correct the issue. It was Sunday, after all. Really, it was the stupidest day for an interview. Then again, that made me more stupid for agreeing to it. (Refer back to Chapter 4.) I looked at my watch knowing I was going to be late. Better not to show up at all, I thought. Much more professional.

I recalled that day so vividly that I almost forgot it was 2020 and I no longer lived in Queens. I was Ms. Hyde all day and eventually I made it to a Starbucks. I should never have left the house. I was a magnet for snags on all sides. I dodged them like I was in a video game. There was even a social distancing protocol, but no one in Palm Beach County seemed to abide by it. No one cared. Granted, it was Florida, but still! The second I got rid of one snag, there would be another one lurking. No one stayed six feet away from me, and I thought to myself, *snags were bad before, now they could make me sick!*

Once I finally got my coffee, a misdirected idiot wearing

his mask around his neck bumped into me. I told him I was going to kill him – right to his face. We were both "technically" wearing surgical masks, so it probably appeared like a pivotal scene on *General Hospital*. Thankfully, he had the good sense to slink away from me. I still think of that jerk when I'm in a bad mood.

That was the first of many times Ms. Hyde reared her ugly head that day. If you find yourself being a Mr. or Ms. Hyde, please realize that doing too much is imprisoning you. Don't leave your apartment or house under these conditions. You're safer inside than braving the elements. Point being, if you get enough sleep this won't be an issue.

Just to further clarify using my earlier example: a well-rested Dr. Jekyll would have bounced out of bed (that's a slight exaggeration – I don't know anyone who bounces out of bed unless the bed's on fire) taken a shower, and remembered the laundromat was closed on Sundays. She would not have locked herself out, and she would have intentionally dressed in the expensive outfit, thinking she'd make it work. She would have been on time for the interview, wowing the dick manager with her bar knowledge and successfully landing the job to prevent her from having to withstand further insulting interrogations regarding her employment.

The rest of her beautiful day would have revolved around doing nothing, most likely drinking at a bar with friends. Try to be Dr. Jekyll at all times. Too many days of being Mr. Hyde is counterproductive.

OK, I'm sure everyone is curious about our favorite pastime, napping. To nap or not to nap, that is the question. Thank you, William Shakespeare. *Hamlet* aside, napping depends on two factors: 1) Is there a safe place for you to do so, and 2) will the nap interfere with the rest of your busy day? Ha ha!

I sometimes spot foolish people picking strange places to nap. The subway, for instance, is a really crack-brained place to fall asleep. How do they know when to wake up? Are they genetically programmed to rouse near their station? I mean, some people win lifetime achievement awards and Pulitzers, but they don't hold a candle to those I've witnessed napping on the D train. These are skilled sleepers, and in my book, that's pretty commendable. In addition, most of them manage not to get robbed. I can only imagine that holding tight to your possessions while sleeping is quite the challenge. Hence, where you take your nap is important.

I'd consider the park risk-free as long as it's in a good neighborhood and you nap during the day. Falling asleep on the beach is acceptable, as long as you've applied layers of strong sunblock and don't suffer from chronic dehydration. If you insist on being outside, a reclining pool chair in the shade is probably your best bet.

Overall, naps are more successful and more easily achieved if they happen indoors. I recommend a bed, but I suppose you could nap on the sofa. Even the plushest of carpets are still rock-hard and tabletops are truly uncomfortable.

Don't even think about catching an informal snooze in a public restaurant or a dark bar. Hecklers have been known to play some sick jokes involving magic marker on people who doze off. The same goes for falling asleep during your doctor's appointment. *How well do you really know your doctor?*

Sidebar #2: When I was fourteen, I worked off the books at my local YMCA, "teaching" swimming to children. You might ask me what this has to do with napping? Well, I'll tell you. I made the job bearable by incorporating naptime into each class. Not only did it provide a quiet moment for me, the kids also seemed to look forward to it. It's not like they enjoyed being wet and cold any more than I did.

I justified naptime by explaining it to the criminals that were running the place in this fashion: The children are visualizing proper stroke technique with their eyes shut. Positive thinking is half the battle, I explained. I encouraged the little devils to lie along the side of the pool's edge, envisioning their arms making clean powerful strokes through the water. At the time, I considered arranging them in what would be perceived as a peace symbol from a satellite view, but the pool deck wasn't wide enough. I stayed dry and did nothing, while keeping my eye on the class in case one of my pupils actually did fall asleep and topple over into the water.

The lesson consisted of ten minutes of naptime, ten minutes of actual swimming, and twenty minutes of water games. Marco Polo was a favorite of mine because the kids couldn't see that I wasn't in the water. The children hopelessly treaded water until they banged into an edge of the pool, and then I'd run to the other side to confuse them.

I managed to stay employed at the YMCA for approximately the same amount of time it took for my

used car to bite the dust. I got the ax when one particularly uptight mother complained about her son's
lack of progress. That was hardly my fault. I personally
think that the naps helped them swim better because
the kids were rejuvenated.

How long to nap is another puzzling question. The "experts," if you will, claim a twenty-minute nap is just as ben-
eficial as a two-hour one. Logically thinking, *how could that
be?* I suggest at least one to two hours. On the other hand, if
you plan on sleeping the entire afternoon away, why get up
in the first place? It's a tough call. Napping for more than a
couple hours is dangerous because it can ruin your chances
for a good night's rest later on. People who are constantly in a
bad mood are sometimes victims of this sequence of events.

Your ultimate goal should be to get enough sleep to work
around your schedule of having to do things. You must be
well rested in order to be extremely clever. Your mind is your
greatest tool when "doing nothing" is the priority.

CHAPTER 15

The Cell Phone — Your True Best Friend

Your cell phone is your best friend. Did I think it would be my BFF twenty years ago? No, but it sure is now. It's critical. Discounting the car, the phone is the most useful tool in the world. Now do remember, cell phones are strictly for calling out, texting, and looking up information. Don't pick it up when it rings. (Unless you've just ordered food. Delivery Dudes sometimes gets lost with your burger deluxe. One time I had a guy call me from 29th Street in Brooklyn, asking my building number. I lived on 29th Street in Manhattan at the time.)

Just to reiterate, it's best to never answer your phone. It creates additional stuff to do. People can't possibly expect a favor if you're unavailable. Speaking of which, the modern day cell phone is imperative for not having to tell people *no way* to their face. Most people are aware of this. One can just text, "No, I can't monitor your turtle's development this upcoming week. I'll be in Bora Bora." You don't have to watch them while they demonstrate on Facetime how lovable a turtle can be.

Basically, if you never answer your phone, you hold all the cards. There are no rules regarding calling someone back. These days if you decide to call a person back, a good chance exists that you'll get their voicemail. Nobody wants to answer the phone because they're either taking my advice, or they like texting better. But when it comes to calling out, why not? It saves you time, makes you look like the better person . . . et cetera. How would you keep a job if you couldn't call to say you won't be there? Showing up and saying you're sick doesn't work when everyone can see you look perfectly fine. Just an aside, staging accidents in person is also rather difficult. Buying an imitation cast and adjusting it properly is no walk in the park.

What do you do when something in your house breaks? I usually stare at it, thinking this can't be happening *again*. I must have gone through fifty lightbulbs and ten appliances in the last year. Lightbulbs you can find easily enough, but legitimate repairmen are almost extinct. Point is, you need your phone. If we couldn't call out, nothing would get fixed.

Phones are also essential for apologies. Cards are even better, but who has time? Apologizing is much easier over the phone. This way you don't have to see the other person's smug look of satisfaction. I so hate that. Saying "sorry" is always hard enough. "I'm sorry I ran away with your best friend," also sounds less serious over the phone. I, personally, like to turn apologies around to make it seem like it's their fault. "I'm sorry you feel that way," has a nice, condescending ring to it.

Phones are crucial for canceling plans. "Sorry, I can't make it," left on their voicemail or text goes a long way. You appear courteous by letting them know. We used to be able to use our health as an excuse when canceling plans. "I don't feel well," brought on compassion rather than fear. Now it simply alarms people, so that subject matter is off limits – and nothing to be joked about.

And once again, hopefully you'll get their voicemail!

Sidebar: The telephone can be useful when asking for favors. In fact, this is the only time we shouldn't mind dialing the people that always pick up their phone. Allow me to provide an example of a phone conversation I had a few years ago from my cell phone in Miami.

I was riding in my friend's car with a couple friends on my way to a club in South Beach when I suddenly realized I'd left my curling iron on in the hotel. Without bothering to mention this small detail to the rest of my rowdy group, I pulled out my cell phone and dialed the hotel.

"The Astor? How may I help you?" a woman's voice echoed back at me as if slightly uncertain of where she was working that day.

"Hi, is everything OK there?" My friend, Suzie, looked up at me quizzically.

"Yes, everything appears to be fine. Who is this?"

"Oh, good! So there's been no fire?"

"Not that I'm aware of. Who is this, again?"

"This is Amy Minty. I'm staying in room three-oh-two."

"What is this call pertaining to, Ms. Minty?" She was suddenly all business like.

"Yeah, I forgot to unplug my curling iron. Could you convince a staff member to go unplug it so the hotel doesn't burn down?"

"Hold on – room three-oh-two, you said?"

"Yes, ma'am." I smiled at Suzie. She gave me a withering look. The hotel receptionist put me on hold for five minutes while I declined hits off multiple joints. Eventually the receptionist came back on the line, and I struggled to hear her over the coughing and shouting going on in the car.

"Ma'am, are you still holding?"

"Yep."

"Your room is no longer a fire threat. I put my best man on it."

I knew she was making fun of me, but I didn't mind. I wondered if her "best man" also rummaged through my belongings looking for cash. Hopefully, he or she wouldn't try on my clothes. "Thank you."

"Oh, and miss, one more thing."

"Yes."

"About twenty years ago they started making curling irons with an automatic shut off. They no longer cause fires. The same goes for any type of iron."

"Really?"

"Really."

"Good to know."

I hung up thinking how cell phones reassure you on so many levels. Every time I think back to all those years living in the city when cell phones didn't exist, I just shake my head. I don't see how we did it – searching for pay phones and relying on answering machines. It boggles my mind. This reminds me of a funny story I'll share with you.

Sidebar #2: As long as you have a phone and a willingness to spend money, anything is possible. An important person, who is now dead, taught me this. He excelled at doing nothing and passed much of his knowledge along to me. He will remain unnamed, but I'm going to call him Paul for the sake of the story.

The only difference between Paul and me was he didn't need sleep to live. He replaced sleeping with gambling. (I wouldn't advise that for the general public. I believe sleep to be a crucial element toward leading a relaxed life, as I pointed out in the last chapter.)

I still lived in NYC at the time. Paul lived in Miami – but he really lived at the Hard Rock Casino in Hollywood – where I was visiting him. Naturally, I extended my trip so long that I ran out of prescription sleeping pills. After a stretch of being awake for forty-eight hours, I went nuts one night. I ranted and raved, broke things, and swilled tequila from the bottle. You know, the usual. I demanded a supply of prescription sleeping pills be delivered to our room at once.

The fact that I had no prescription was not the problem. Paul had plenty of "doctor friends," and Collins Avenue was only forty minutes away if we went the unconventional route. The dilemma was that pharmacies were either closed or wouldn't deliver after ten p.m. This enraged me. The only drugstore even open at midnight was half an hour away by car.

Anyway, this is what we did. We used Paul's cell to call a limousine service and requested their assistance. We didn't intend to get the pills ourselves (that would require leaving the casino), so after a brief chat with the company, we figured out a solution.

When the driver, Carlos, arrived at our hotel, he said he required a credit card to go pick up the prescription that was in Paul's name. Apparently, Carlos had done this before. Neither Paul nor I owned a credit card of any type. We just laughed; it wasn't even an option. We paid for everything in cash.

"Do you have a credit card?" Paul asked Carlos.

"Yes," he replied. (Whether it was really his, we'll never know.)

"OK, use your card to pay for it. I'll have the prescription put in your name," Paul said.

Carlos nodded slowly.

"Do you understand?" Paul asked. "Pay for our stuff with your card and we'll give you cash when you get back. It will be worth your while. Got it?"

Carlos nodded again, and took the written instructions on how to get to the only twenty-four hour pharmacy in Miami. "OK," he said.

The door shut behind him. "I hope this works," I said. "Carlos seemed a little confused. He might come back with a handful of Sominex that we could have easily bought in the lobby of this hotel." I continued to swill tequila.

About an hour or so later, Carlos knocked on our

door and handed me a full prescription of Xanax. His other hand was extended palm up. Carlos was rewarded nicely, and I finally got some sleep.

The point of my story is a single phone call had allowed us to hire Carlos, complete with his own transportation, to use his own credit card in order to pick up drugs for us. If Carlos had said no, we would have phoned someone else who would have agreed to our wishes.

Without a phone, we could have done none of this.

CHAPTER 16

Ways To Avoid Doing Things

I can't speak for everyone, but full agendas make me panic. (Granted, these days, I'd give anything to have a full agenda, without it being Zoomed from my living room.) Nor, is the reluctance I feel to meet certain demands a recent phenomenon. Since I can remember, anytime I've had something I *had* to do, the tendency to procrastinate has always been there. Before online banking, the majority of my bills went unpaid, not because I was broke, but because it was such a pain in the butt to write a check and find a stamp. I spent almost my whole life procrastinating before I realized I could avoid doing things completely.

I am a person who suffers from recurring nightmares. My most common nightmare takes me back to my childhood, in which I've left it to the last minute to read and learn 1600 pages of World History. (I obviously have some deep-rooted fear of going back to school. School, to the best of my recollection, was just one big building that I visited at random. In college, there was more than one building, but it was the same idea.) This particular dream signifies that I have molded my life around procrastination. I thought everyone felt like I did, but then I went and married Ron Kochman, so I know this not to be the case. (We will try to keep him out of this book as much as possible, but let's just say for the record, some people don't procrastinate.) However, for those of us who take stalling to new heights, dodging every day activities in order to do nothing begins at an early age. Which kid ever liked to brush his teeth? Or liked being told to go to bed? A typical child's life revolves around avoiding school and dodging the doctor and the dentist. Kids are instinctually smart. They complain and do anything in their power to avoid going to places they don't want to go and doing things they don't enjoy.

This early learning process continues through high school, at least for us raised in America. We prolong searching for the after-school job and any form of babysitting. To my early chagrin, I was *almost* a kid with a paper route. Although my father was big on instilling a hard working ethic, he was not keen about the amount of crime in our neighborhood. Basically, I got lucky in my unlucky circumstances. At least I avoided that embarrassment.

After completing high school, avoiding college appealed to me too, but the alternative was working full-time. Working full-time *anywhere* sounded like a lot of effort. I opted for college out of sheer desperation and my mother's eagerness for me to appear smart. I thought college would provide an ongoing supply of parties and delay permanent employment by four years. Wrong, again. Tuition, rent, food, transportation, clothing, alcohol, books for my classes – the costs were endless. Obviously, something had to give. After my first year of college, I stopped buying books. What was the point in buying a book you never opened? Sure, my grades weren't top honors, but who cared as long as I graduated?

The bottom line is paying for college is hard. I was tricked. I went to school and still had to work forty hours a week. Hence, learning ways to avoid doing things became my biggest passion and greatest skill. One I continue to excel at. The truth is, from an early age I hated participating in obligatory duties. I'm sure I was not alone. Finally, I realized there were steps I could take to reduce my participation. I figured out ways around having to do the things I didn't want to. I have also learned to procrastinate less by simply avoiding an undesirable task altogether.

Being skillful and resourceful can aid you in your mission of avoiding responsibilities, as you learned in the previous chapter. For example, when it's time to do your taxes, don't wait until mid-April to consider your options. Get it out of the way in February while people are running around like morons buying roses for Valentine's Day. Now don't get me wrong – I'm not suggesting you try to make sense of those confusing tax forms. Pay someone to do it. Very simple. No hassle, less procrastination, and it's done.

The most obvious category associated with chronic avoidance is the routine things we secretly hate doing. Everyone hates something different. For instance, I don't like to wash dishes. So I rarely dirty them. If you despise something, I strongly urge you not to do it. If it drives you crazy to mow the lawn, don't! Landscapers can do that for you even if your plot of land is no bigger than your living room. On a weekly basis, it will cost less than maintaining a decent lawnmower.

Sidebar: As adults, I insist you make decisions for yourselves; as kids, we didn't always have a choice. I grew up in a family that made me do chores. OK – I'm emotionally scarred – I'll admit it. I don't know if chores still exist among American families anymore, but I seriously doubt it.

Winter was rough in Massachusetts, and we were the only family in Worcester that still used a hardwood fire to heat our house. Coal was readily available back then; it was just a matter of choice. My father's choice became another one of my chores. Spending the afternoon piling firewood was a winter constant. I still shiver when I think about it. (I will elaborate more on this in Chapter 18.)

At some point during sixth grade, my friends and I began experimenting with smoking. All the kids in the neighborhood used to hide their cigarettes down near the bottom of one of our massive woodpiles. Discovery didn't seem high risk. One would think . . .

One night before supper, my father came across a pack of Lucky Strikes. During the meal, he proceeded to rant and rave about our degenerate high school neighbors hiding various carcinogens on our property. My girlfriend – who happened to stay over for dinner that night – and I had been smoking from that pack all week. We both coughed out our soup at the same time, claiming it was very hot.

I repeat: Do not do things you hate! Find a way around it. Life is too short! You don't need a reason! Just refuse –

it's your personal right. It all boils down to what you do and what you don't do. For the most part, excuses are wasted on people, but it makes us feel justified in our actions. Assuming you decide against doing something, you may want to have a reason ready that is believable. Here are some sample future phone calls…

- I've been kidnapped . . . No, I wouldn't joke about this . . . Sorry I won't be able to make the pickling and canning workshop!
- I had to go out of town. The Smith's will throw another curry party, won't they?
- I'm working on an oil painting . . . Yes, they still exist . . . No, if the paint dries, there's no going back. . . You don't understand. There won't be a tomorrow for these seagulls in flight. I'll catch your opening night the next time around.
- I'm stuck in an elevator . . . I know, these cell phones are great, aren't they? They work anywhere . . . Ugh, I really hate to miss your daughter's school play.
- I'm in jail . . . Yes, really, it's a long story . . . You're my one phone call . . . Obviously, it's a misunderstanding . . . no, a bit more serious than that. They think I killed someone. It's safe to say, I'm going to miss Bob's surprise party.

You get the drift. Make up anything you want if you feel you need an excuse. Religion is another great alibi (even if you've never worshipped in your life). Since religion can be quite competitive, it can provide the perfect rescue. If you have to go to church, you have to go to church. Who an earth is going to argue with that? So people will begin to think you're a religious zealot, but so what? Who cares? They'll change their mind when they run into you out on the town, partying like a rock star. Watching you booze it up, while ripping up the dance floor, will cause them to disbelieve any previous religious excuses that rolled off your tongue. But by that time it's too late. You've successfully dodged the event you wanted to avoid.

Also, pretending to be a different religion from the specific sacred event you're sidestepping can free you from the obligatory duty. Example: Claiming Jewish descent, you are now exempt from joining your friends at Midnight Mass. You also won't have to pretend to enjoy Easter. (There's only one "bunny" we've ever liked anyway, and it's not the Easter bunny.)

What about lent? That's the best excuse of all time. You could say you have given up anything for forty days. Some people sacrifice things they actually enjoy in the name of lent. What's the point of that? God has plenty of unpleasant surprises planned for us as it is. The year 2020 is a perfect example. Haven't we sacrificed enough?

I may have suggested some effective excuses that aid in our quest to avoid doing things, but telling the truth is another option. When people ask me to join them on the ski slopes in Vail, I say, "No way. I hate skiing." When they ask me why, I give the real reason. "It's too cold, and I'm not good at it." Keep it simple. Another added bonus to telling the truth is they won't ask you again. All my real friends know I hate period films. And guess what? They still like me even though I won't sit down and watch *The Favourite* with them.

Eventually, even the smoothest talker runs out of excuses. It's even happened to me. Once, I didn't want to endure a lecture on thoroughbred racehorses, so I said I broke my foot. I then had to arrive everywhere with crutches for the next two months, and the excuse was definitely not worth it. In addition, last minute excuses generally lead to outright lies, and sometimes it's difficult to remember them all. It's exhausting to recall what you told whom and when. My suggestion is to remain consistent in your lies in order to avoid confusion down the road.

I'm a terrible liar. Don't get me wrong, I lie easily, I'm just bad at it. Once upon a time, I told Laurent at Flask that an emergency trip to Spain had come up. (At the time, I didn't even know where Spain was located on a map of the world. Remember, geography is not my strong suit.) There was a music festival going on at Madison Square Garden, and I was planning to be there every night for a week. The shows were fantastic, and I spent the following few nights after recovering in my local bar. I never thought about Spain once. When I finally went back to work and the staff at Flask asked me how my trip was I said, "Fantastic concerts – yeah." Realizing my mistake, I followed it up with, "There's some great live music in Spain." I had to change the subject very quickly. There's nothing worse than having to do research to support a lie.

Sidebar #2: While on the subject of lying, my mother and I once made a rather annoying mistake. On a trip to visit my grandparents (on my father's side), we told them that we didn't eat dairy products. My grandmother had a habit of force-feeding her family rice pudding and cream-laden dishes all day. As far as her cooking went, she somehow managed to incorporate half-and-half into just about every meal.

However, my grandmother was an extremely sharp woman. It's actually safe to say she was more astute and smarter than my mother and me combined. So when Sarah Minty and I began slathering butter on our bread and pouring milk in our coffee, we should have known we'd be busted. When the brie and crackers hit the table (our favorite cheese), our gig was officially up. My mother and I learned from our error. We should have specified we were opposed to cream. Consider your excuse or lie from all angles before committing to it.

Temporary situation lies are always better than long-term lies. Had my mother and I not been so daft, we would have had to avoid dairy products around my grandmother for the next twenty years. (More on my mother in the following chapter.) The honest truth, no matter how insensitive it is, is usually better than a long-term lie you have to live with.

CHAPTER 17

Doing Nothing:
Does It Come Down To Genetics?

Genetics: the study of heredity and the variation of inherited characteristics.

Webster's definition is a little bit too technical for me, but as I sit here scratching my head, one thing is abundantly clear. As far as having the inclination to do nothing, I don't have to be a biologist to know I take after my mother and her side of the family.

In the glorious days of my youth, my mother never wanted to do a darn thing, and I believe her ancestors felt the same. From what I understand, never having met my grandmother on my mother's side, there was a farm involved, and it didn't sound like the women did much work. I don't even think they cooked what the men killed for dinner. In truth, my mother can't recall anything other than riding her horse to the nearest ranch where kegs of beer and whiskey were so copious they were considered crops.

To this day, there is a beautiful photograph of my great-grandmother in her nineties resting on my mother's desk. She is smoking a cigarette, surrounded by empty bottles of champagne and dozens of boxes of chocolates. That photo is the most inspiring heirloom in my family. Let's hear it for genetics!

It is obvious that my mother, her mother, and her grandmother perfected doing nothing long before I was ever born. And one would think, aren't those genetically predisposed to doing nothing have an edge? Genetics must at least *contribute* to the mechanics behind our personality.

My aunt Candy was another perfect example of a woman who excelled at doing nothing. Naturally, she was on my mother's side of the family. She was, technically, my mother's cousin, but close enough to me that she deserved a finer title. She lived in London and managed a hotel. She hated working and loved to visit America to see my mother and vacation. When in town, she would stay in Manhattan, either at the Carlisle or the Plaza, and the first thing we'd do upon her arrival was race over to Cipriani across the street. The bellman hadn't even delivered her luggage to the room before we were nestled into a dark booth, sipping Bellinis. We'd snack on caviar and foie gras for fortitude as we geared up to spend a month of paychecks at Bloomingdale's. Candy lived to have fun, and she prioritized the four exceptions to the rules.

I had a strange balance growing up. My father was dedicated and determined and hard-working. (I will discuss the impact of learned behavior, and the result of a militant upbringing, in the following chapter.) He was always working and continuously traveling, but my mother stayed home and never wanted to drive us kids anywhere. My mother's lackluster approach to almost everything remained consistent to the day I moved out of the house. At the time, I was too young and too annoyed with her to applaud her ultimate wisdom, but the years that followed proved she was right all along. I'll provide you with a couple of routine example conversations:

"Mom, I want to go to the football game at school. Everyone's going to be there," I said.

"Oh, yeah? Who do you think has to drive you?" she hissed.

"Ma, it'll take ten minutes," I pleaded.

"That's not the point. Who do you think has to pick you up as well?"

"I'll get a ride home."

"How do you know that? What if you can't? Will my whole evening revolve around taking you to a *sporting event*?"

"What were you planning on doing?" I wailed.

"Absolutely nothing, but that doesn't mean I have to live my life around my kids."

***

"Ma, can I take gymnastics?"

"Where?"

"This place off the highway. It's like five minutes away."

"When?"

"Tuesdays at five."

"No."

"Why not?"

"Not unless you want to walk, and I won't have you walking along the highway."

Looking back, it was actually a good thing she saved me

from that unnatural bending of the body, but I do think I was the youngest kid ever to buy my own car. I bought it before I even had a driver's license. It was a used Dodge Daytona I purchased from the owner of a gas station, and barely operable, but it got me from point A to point B. (As I was driving, exterior parts used to fall off and hit surrounding vehicles.)

Being as my mother did so little in my youth, I had no idea what she actually enjoyed. In my twenties, I was able to ascertain that she seemed to like vacationing and movies, minimal shopping and dining out. As I grew older and infinitely wiser, I realized that my mother and I are two peas from the same jaded pod. Now we love to do nothing together. Unfortunately, we live on different continents, so doing nothing with each other is currently on hold, but will be resumed as soon as humanly possible.

Sidebar: When my mother lived in South Jersey and I lived in Manhattan, we used to meet halfway, in Princeton, NJ. We loved to loiter there because it was considered such a "nice town." (Anywhere the community gathers regularly at an old-fashioned ice cream shop fits the profile.)

My mother would pick me up at the Hamilton train station, and we would always get lost trying to find Princeton. These were the days before GPS and cell phones, and every road was familiar because we'd taken so many of the same wrong turns.

This particular afternoon she arrived in a Chevy Impala. Considering she normally drove a white Honda Civic, you'd think she would have gotten out of the car to wave me over in her direction once the train arrived, but no. Unable to locate her, and not seeing her, I began looking in every car window. Finally, I caught a glimpse of her little head just barely peeking over the massive steering wheel of this random, sinister-looking automobile. Her nose buried deep in a novel, I startled Sarah Minty by knocking on the window.

She struggled to wind down the window manually. The car had to have been from the eighties, before the invention of power windows and electronic features. "Hiya," she said, like nothing was out of the ordinary.

"How exactly did you think I was going to find you?" I asked, climbing into the passenger seat.

"Whatcha mean?"

"I mean, whose car is this? And why are you driving it?"

"Oh, silly me. Brian Weiss has me so mesmerized. He knows."

I glanced at the new age cover of the book she was reading. "Knows what?"

"Oh, Amy. He's so spiritual." My mother had a wistful look in her eyes.

"I don't care about Brian Weiss. Not at this moment anyway. Whose car is this? Where is your shit car?" I repeated.

"Oh, it's a long story, darling. Mine's in the shop. This is Jimmy's car."

"Who the fuck is Jimmy?"

"Oh, you know, my neighbor. He lives in the teal-colored house with all those mermaid sculptures out front. Honestly, I wish he'd mow his lawn more often. Makes the entire block look bad. Anyway, he helped me paint the rainbow scheme in the den. You met him at last year's Fourth of July barbeque."

"I did?"

"Yes, you had that horrible orange spray tan, so you let him hose you down in the backyard. Remember?"

"Vaguely. What's wrong with your car – besides the fact it's a Honda."

"Oh, I backed into a tree leaving 7-Eleven. It was dark, and the tree came out of nowhere."

"I hate it when that happens."

"It was a big tree. Eight hundred dollars large."

"Is your car even worth that much?"

Sarah seemed to consider this question before admitting, "I'm not sure."

"How was your day otherwise?"

"Fantastic!"

"How so?" My mother was working as an occupational therapist for children in North Philly at the time, and she never said her day was even remotely good.

"I've done so little all day!" she exclaimed. You could tell she was pleased. She was already zooming down the wrong street in the wrong direction.

I smiled.

"My first child canceled, which was marvelous, and my second kid was twenty minutes late, which cut his time short. My third patient wanted to reschedule, so basically, I just drove this car around all day, listening to Enya. It was a thoroughly enjoyable afternoon apart from when I had lunch at Carvel."

"Carvel. The always-about-to-go-out-of-business ice cream shop?"

"Yes. It's divine. I often lunch there. But today, this shady character mistook this gas guzzler for his drug dealer's, and came up to my window holding a brown envelope that I could only assume contained cash. I was so surprised, I laughed at first – I even considered taking it and peeling away, but then I decided better of it. But, truth be told, I'm kind of regretting my decision."

And then we were officially off, soaring down the road in hot pursuit of the nearest restroom. Our priorities were loosely based, and the first stop was always finding the closest bathroom.

We stopped at a place called "The Rusty Scupper," a dark, eerie, seafood house that reeked of criminal activity. Finally, we fit in, parking next to the other Chevy Impalas and Oldsmobiles. This wasn't our first rodeo at "The Rusty Scupper." My mother and I never actually ate there. We just used the washroom every chance we got.

Jumping back into the Chevy, we drove around in additional circles until we made it to Princeton. We parked in the easiest lot, began to wander around, and embraced the fact we had nothing to do.

Our first stop was the toy store. Toys are super inventions. It's simply too bad I can't think of a great new toy before someone else beats me to it. Naturally, the shop was filled with adults. Probably only a small percentage of them had kids they were shopping for. There was only one small boy in the store. He was playing on the floor with a cooking set, and he seemed to have no attachment to any particular adult.

"Oh look." Sarah pointed to him. "That was probably Vince as a child. God bless him." She was referring to the fact my ex-husband was a chef.

"Vince didn't grow up in an academic setting like Princeton, mom. This child is probably wondering why the oven isn't getting hot." I reached for a yo-yo hanging from a nearby shelf.

"I wonder if they have face painting kits here," Sarah murmured, veering off. I didn't bother to ask. For all I knew, my mother was decorating her face and practicing Shamanism in her spare time. *Good for her*, I thought absentmindedly, searching for a salesgirl.

I trapped this particular victim in one of the sixteen corners of the store. Awkward space, but I knew it like the back of my hand. (Mom and Pop toy stores tend to be small, the isles usually tight.) At any rate, this sales girl appeared to be roughly fifteen with braces and a large nametag.

"Eugenia, do you sell acrylic paint-by-numbers here?"

"I know we have watercolor."

"That's not what I asked."

"You don't want watercolor?"

"No."

"How old is the child you're shopping for?" Eugenia asked.

"Twenty-seven. She doesn't want to think, she just

wants to paint."

"I see." Eugenia led me to a small stack of acrylic paint-by-numbers. The pictures were boring. Mountains and triple-story houses and bowls of fruit. One was a bunch of horses stranded in a field. The type of pictures that eventually wound up in a large dumpster.

"I was looking for something a bit more fun," I confessed.

"It's a family shop in *Princeton*," she hissed. "Try Manhattan for something edgier."

"Right," I said. "Good advice." As I'd just traveled from there, I didn't particularly appreciate her sarcasm.

I found my mom. She was holding a bead-your-own-lamp. "Do you think this is safe?" she asked. "Lightbulbs can get quite hot."

"I have no idea. Let's go before I murder the salesgirl."

Sarah and I continued to shop idly and with no focus, eventually making a beeline for the Lindt chocolate store. It was inevitable, of course. I had just spent thousands of dollars fixing my teeth. Naturally, I wanted to consume as much sugar as possible.

"Look, free samples for us," Sarah said, quickly unwrapping a pink-wrapped candy from a Mother's Day basket by the door. (There was no sign to indicate they were free.) I noticed the lady behind the counter eyeing us up as potential troublemakers, so I bought a pound of dark chocolate balls to restore our upstanding reputation.

Thrilled with all the time we'd wasted, we settled

into a table at our favorite Mediterranean restaurant. It boasted a variety of fresh fish which always pleased my mother. I requested Robert, our favorite waiter, and a wine list. Robert spotted us and sauntered over, rolling his eyes. "How are you ladies this lovely spring evening? You're both looking marvelous."

Sarah and I smirked feeling smug and appreciated. My mother spoke first. "See Amy, I love Robert. Even though he smiles at you all night long, he takes the time to glance in my direction. He doesn't ignore me completely. Are there any specials tonight, Robert?"

Winking at me, Robert read off the specials and took our drink order. My mother waited until he'd left to ask me about the fish of the day. "What's tilapia, Amy?"

"You won't like it. Stick to the salmon."

"What does it taste like?"

I set down my menu. "To be honest, it tastes like dirt."

"How do you know what dirt tastes like?"

"I'd rather not get into it. I just know you won't like it."

"But I've never tried it!"

"For good reason."

"Is it an oily fish, Amy?"

"Not particularly."

"My dermatologist says oily fish is good for my skin."

"See, even more reason to order the salmon."

"How do you even know about this fish?"

"We served it in Vince's restaurant once. I'll never forget the complaints."

Robert returned with our martinis. "What's the preparation with the tilapia, Robert?" Sarah asked.

He gave me an uneasy look. "Umm . . . no one has actually ordered it yet, but it's filleted and served atop sweet potato puree and collard greens in traditional Louisiana bayou style."

"Ooh delish! I'm sold!" Sarah announced.

Robert looked at me for confirmation.

I nodded. "It's like throwing thirty bucks in the river."

"OK," Robert said, making a note in his pad. "Sarah, would you like it grilled, fried, or blackened? I suggest double blackened to remove any potential bacteria."

"Oh, Robert. You're a hoot! Double blackened then," Sarah said, taking a swig of her martini. She was not big on cheering.

Robert turned to me. "Amy, your normal filet mignon, walking rare, extra garlic butter with your normal sides?"

"Yep, thanks. Does the chef have a friend in Louisiana?" I asked.

"Kentucky," he said with disdain. "Last week we had catfish on the menu. We toted it as the poor man's seabass, but our customers were not convinced. Thank goodness our clientele is smarter than the owners of this actual establishment."

Twenty minutes later, Sarah and I had gobbled up our oysters, a bottle of wine was opened and poured, and one order of tilapia was exchanged for an order of grilled salmon.

Still enjoying doing nothing, we finished our meal then walked over to get dessert at a nearby café. Before leaving we hit the bathroom for the tenth time. Doing a lot of nothing inspires drinking a lot, hence, chances to peruse many restrooms in different locations. My next book should be an encyclopedia on "powder rooms" in the United States. Like a Zagat's with ratings and driving directions. God knows I've done my research.

This particular restroom was a one-person stall and Sarah and I were crowded in there together like two rats in a tin can. I took out my pen to jot down a note, while my mom was crouching over the toilet. Perhaps it was a strange time to remember something I had to do, but my mom looked up and saw me holding a pen. "I hope you're not sketching me!" she cried.

In the final analysis, my mother is one of my favorite people to do nothing with. Heredity or not, we think alike. The more family you can engage in this fun-spirited activity, the better. Even if you don't have my blessed lineage, do not let this derail you from living the easiest life possible. Remember, doing nothing is a *technique*, and can be learned and mastered.

CHAPTER 18

Do Upbringing And Learned Behavior Play A Part In The Urge To Do Nothing?

What makes us long to do nothing? Or the opposite: what drives us to be productive and successful? Does our upbringing impact our thinking? Are our actions dependent on what we have or have not been subjected to? In this chapter, I plan to flush out just how much impact the circumstances surrounding how we are raised can have on our psyche.

I mentioned my father in the previous chapter. He was a clear-cut example of being driven to work hard. My father, the eldest of four growing up in England in the fifties, bore the most responsibility to help contribute to the family's finances from an early age. This was largely due to my grandmother's influence.

As long as I can remember, my father's mother, Margaret Minty, attempted to instill the hardworking ethic into her rather uncooperative grandchildren. My grandmother would call on the phone and my mother would have to battle the fiery questioning. "Are the kids working, Sarah? Are they helping to pay the bills?"

My sister and I were nine and twelve at the time.

"You do understand that we can pay the bills, right? Michael and I."

"I should hope so, but the kids should be contributing!"

"Well, they're not eligible for real jobs yet – it's still illegal. But Amy's babysitting and Fay is really pulling her weight around the house," my mother would gush, glancing around at the mess while frowning at my sister and me sacked out in front of the TV. "They just love to help out."

My sister and I would look at each other for a brief moment and roll our eyes in unison, knowing instantly who had phoned. Then we would focus our attention back on *Three's Company* or *Too Close for Comfort*. Babysitting? Never heard of it. (This temporary relaxation, of course, only lasted until my father would arrive home from work.)

Through the years, my grandmother continued to shove her work ethic in my face. In high school, I once told her I was stealing as much cash as possible from the register at the local truck stop where I worked, and she genuinely smiled, her demeanor instantly brightening. "Good for you. Keep it up!" she effused.

My grandmother understood business. When I moved to New York City shortly after high school, Margaret Minty was thrilled to hear I was working as a shot girl at the Palladium. She had no clue what being a shot girl entailed, nor did she have any clue that the Palladium was a cavernous drug-fueled club that hosted a rave every night. I was raking in the bucks; Margaret was thrilled. More excited than I, unfortunately. I was eighteen. I shouldn't have even been selling liquor, much less working from ten at night until six in the morning, but all my grandmother cared about was the almighty dollar. If you were an earner, you were a winner!

But let's back up, shall we? It's rather doubtful that Margaret was born with this fierce determination to accumulate as much money as possible. It is my belief that circumstances molded her along the way. I'm going to use her as an example and expand upon her upbringing in order to highlight how one's environment is vital to one's thinking. In order to do this, I must provide some background information.

The second oldest of five kids, Margaret was born in Germany to Benjamin and Katherine. Benjamin was British and met Katherine during World War I in Germany. They married and proceeded to stay in Germany until 1938 when Adolf Hitler's actions "forced" them to leave. At the time, Ben owned a motorcycle shop. He sold and repaired Bonneville motorcycles – now called Triumph. Apparently, their motorcycles were used largely in the game of motoball, which is the game of soccer, but played on your motorcycle with an oversized ball. (If you can imagine such a thing.) This was an extremely popular sport in Germany at the time, and my great-grandfather's business contributed to Triumph's long-term success.

My grandmother could not have been older than fourteen or fifteen before Ben demanded his daughters run errands for the business. I was told this was not an option, and Margaret had to learn how to ride a motorbike at an early age in order to make frequent trips to the registry to submit paperwork for the purchases and sales of bikes. This was still prior to World War II, but Hitler was gearing up for the war. He requisitioned all motorcycles, taking them for military use, preparing Germany to become a superpower at Margaret's family's expense. Ben was then relegated to only bike repair. That is, until Hitler banned all imports coming into Germany, which resulted in Ben's inability to receive motorcycle parts. So now Ben could no longer sell or repair motorcycles. He had three daughters, a young son, and a wife to support, so he began speaking out against the government.

From what I understand, his protesting backfired. Germany had not yet invaded Poland, but Hitler was already placing people who didn't fit Hitler's Aryan mold in concentration camps. Ben discovered he'd been added to the list. He quickly fled to his native land of England, leaving Germany with nothing. His wife and four kids followed shortly thereafter.

Like many refugees, life was hard on my grandmother and her two sisters. They spoke no English, but upon arriving in England, the girls got jobs at a hotel, working room service as kitchen help, and learning the language. My grandmother was still fifteen. Once Margaret and her sisters learned to speak English well enough, and the war spread to England, they were able to graduate to employment in a factory that built aircraft for the war. After working ten-hour days on an assembly line, Margaret and her older sister were also assigned to the nightly fire watch – a voluntary, yet necessary duty. Sitting on the roof of their home, they were responsible for watching for fires that would erupt in the wee hours after the bombs were dropped on London's neighborhoods. Everyone was responsible for the safety of their own neighborhood.

Margaret Minty was a product of her environment. She might have been very different if she'd grown up in Texas with an oil baron for a father. Margaret's parents were forced to flee Germany and start over in England. Everyone in the family worked, and they worked hard. *Are you seeing where I'm going with this?*

Ben, upon arriving in England, began a car-for-hire business, and became successful enough to purchase a gas station. Ben sold gas, fixed cars, and added a metal plating and finishing component to his enterprise. In 1940, Margaret met my grandfather, Albert, who was soon to be a British soldier.

When World War II ended in 1945, there were few jobs for ex-combatants, so Albert went to work for Ben at his newly purchased gas station. Albert continued working for Ben, and in 1946 my grandmother gave birth to my father. The question that looms is whether or not my father was genetically predisposed to being a hard worker or was he raised to be that way? Being the eldest of four children, born to a mother with a strong German work ethic doesn't leave much room for speculation.

Since my father died many years ago, much of this information pertaining to my great-grandparents and grandparents has been provided to me by my Aunt Jan, my father's youngest sister. She recalls Margaret being the driving force as far as pushing my father to earn as much money as he could. According to Jan, my father had a paper route at the age of nine. In addition to sports and school, he also repackaged huge sacks of potatoes, then sold and delivered them in smaller quantities to nearby neighborhoods. I was told this little entrepreneurial endeavor was a niche my father devised because few people had cars in London, and potatoes were heavy to lug back home from the market. Families were willing to pay a little extra to get such items brought directly to their homes.

When I asked Jan whether my grandfather, Albert, was

driven, or at the very least, ambitious, it took her a few seconds to respond. "I think he was fine with just plodding along," she finally said. *I have a feeling my grandfather would have loved this book!* So, clearly my father learned from his mother, and not his father, how to "bust his ass." I'm assuming he had very little choice in the matter, but I wasn't there, so I can't be a hundred percent sure.

Just to complete the timeline and reinforce how hardworking Margaret Minty was, here is the rest of the story. . .

Margaret and Albert eventually decided to emigrate to America. My grandparents were in their forties and unable to purchase a house in England due to their age. Amazingly, if you were over 45 years old at that time in England, you could no longer qualify for a mortgage. In America, there were no such restrictions.

Settling in Massachusetts, my grandmother went to work at Norton's, an abrasives manufacturing company. She was assigned to the diamond tool division, and proceeded to shave and cut automotive instruments for the next twenty years. When Norton's was eventually bought out by a French company in 1990, she was forced to retire. She was in her mid-sixties. There is no doubt in my mind she would have kept working well into her seventies or longer if given the choice.

My grandfather, Albert, on the other hand, who had learned his trade of metal finishing and plating from Margaret's father, Ben, retired the second he could justify it. I remember going over to their house in Leicester, Mass., as a child, and experienced my grandfather watching football, drinking beer and cracking nuts with breathtaking speed, while my grandmother was still at work. The shag carpet was a mess of walnut casings and pecan shells. When my grandmother got home from her shift at the factory, which included overtime, he'd immediately ask when dinner was going to be ready. You get the picture . . .

Years later, once Norton's was no more, Albert convinced Margaret to move to North Carolina, where he could play tennis year-round.

I think I have successfully outlined one of the main reasons MY father was so driven: my grandmother instilled a hard work ethic in him, and I do believe, in this case, his work ethic was learned, as opposed to genetic.

My father attempted to instill the same principles in my sister and me. That worked really well. NOT. Obviously, at the time, we did what we were told because we had no choice. I was older, lucky me, so I had it worse. My father often used to look me up and down, sizing me up like one would assess a racehorse's capabilities, seeing just how adept I might be at physical labor. He'd squint at my out-of-shape frame, wondering just how much weight I might be able to lift, while he calculated my level of stamina and coordination. I especially remember him doing this during the winters, right before he'd take me out to the backyard and hand me the ax. The first year he did this, I recall holding it awkwardly and wondering how I was going to lift it over my head, much less split a log.

I did what I was told. I raised the ax as high as possible and brought it down as hard as I could, splintering the wood to the best of my ability. I did this again and again until there was just a mass of haphazard pieces scattered on our lawn, which I then had to pick up and stack. And stacking wasn't easy, since every piece ranged in size. When you buy firewood at Home Depot it's fairly uniform. It's hardly consistent when your ten-year-old daughter is running the show. I suppose I was cheap labor, so he could overlook the imperfections. After all, he wasn't the one stacking it all day.

During the years that followed, I simply stared miserably at the various fallen trees that my father had hacked down from our mass of woods in the backyard while he reminded me to use proper form. *Aim for the center of the log surface!* This advice was not to prevent personal injury, but to ensure a more even split down the middle of the log.

There is also a caveat to this. On rainy and snowy days, which was almost all winter long in Massachusetts, those carefully stacked woodpiles had to be transferred into the garage to stay dry. Somehow this also became my responsibility. However, since I could only carry one or two logs at a time, this project required two men. (Or in my case, one man and one child.) I would hold my arms out and my father would stack as many logs in my arms that I could carry without keeling over. Then I'd trudge back and forth from the backyard to the garage until we were done. Such fond memories I have of those bitterly windy and cold nights.

Winters were indeed the worst, as chopping, piling, and transferring wood was just one of my obligatory duties. For those of you who had the luxury of growing up in a year-round warm climate, and are unaware of this fact: snow does not shovel itself. Nor does it melt that quickly or easily. I was on driveway duty from October to April. (Don't let anyone tell you it doesn't snow up north in late fall or early spring. It does.)

I can remember snow days when all my friends would be sledding while I hopelessly shoveled the two feet of snow and sleet in our driveway. There's nothing worse than scooping heaps of heavy ice-caked slush after the sun has gone down. My parents refused to invest in anything electric or gas powered to remove snow from our property. It was just me and the red shovel. My back would ache and my gloves were routinely miniature ice sculptures. I almost dug my own grave one cold December day. Frostbite declared war on my hands. That was fun. It took me four hours for my fingers to thaw, and I didn't speak to my parents until the following year. You might ask where my father was during these lovely afternoons? At work, always working, content with the knowledge that he was helping Amy build character at home, while my mother was eating bonbons on the couch, cradling her hot chocolate for warmth in our frigid house.

Back in the early eighties, my father paid me three dollars for this inhumane task of shoveling our driveway. This worked out to be about twenty-five cents an hour. The money was supposed to be my incentive, but I clearly don't remember having a say in the matter. I would have much preferred risking the dangers of sledding with my foolhardy friends.

Now this doesn't mean I was let off the hook come summertime. Oh no. There was still plenty of yard and house maintenance to address as my father attempted to "instill good values" in me. (Little did he know that the end result would be me writing an entire book about doing nothing.)

To this day, I'm still convinced that the reason my father bought so much land was because they had *me* to mow it with a push mower, and I'm certain the reason my mother planted so many flowers and plants was because they had *me* to weed the steep, cliff-like embankment, which was our backyard. In addition, I know without a shadow of a doubt, that we never had the driveway paved, because they had me pour additional bags of rocks each summer to replace the ones I'd dug up with the shovel during the winter. And then rake the rocks so the driveway *appeared* even. (No wonder my father drove a four-wheel drive Toyota.)

And then there was *inside* the house. If it seemed I was being idle for a second, my mother, while reading *Vogue* and stirring something inedible on the stove would suggest, "Why don't you go clean behind the furniture?"

"But no one sees behind the furniture," I'd protest.

"That doesn't mean it doesn't get dusty like everything else."

But here's the thing, with my mother it was different. She wasn't trying to make a hard worker out of me. She just wanted me out of her hair, and she didn't want to have to do such things, which I totally respect now. (Refer back to Chapter 17 for more specifics.) So basically, apart from my father screaming at me to clean the dishes, vacuum the rugs and mop the floor, my manual labor was mostly contained to backbreaking, physical, outdoor duties. Yes, I blame my grandmother and her side of the family. My father's learned behavior was their fault and eventually became my problem.

Let's talk about the effect this had on me as an adult: *I do not take after my father.* Unfortunately, I had to work very hard in my life to get where I am today. But as you've read so far in this book, I've chosen the path of least resistance and perfected ways to give the impression I was hard working, when truly all I wanted to do was participate in the four exceptions to the rules.

Needless to say, learned behavior played a huge part in my urge to do nothing. When I moved to the city, I knew

I would never mow another lawn as long as I lived. I also hoped I would never have to pick up another ax unless I was starring in a horror film. I avoided all housework and cleaning, and I never learned how to cook. I've basically been on strike since the age of sixteen. That doesn't mean I didn't work long hours and had to support myself. I did, but I did it in ways I could handle.

Then there is the flip side: if a kid views his or her parents as lazy couch potatoes, he or she might get the wrong idea. Never witnessing the alternative, a child of such blessed lineage might misunderstand the importance of doing nothing. The confused adolescent might even jump to the false conclusion that being successful and productive is the goal. He or she might lose focus when it comes to finding happiness while doing less.

So, there you have it. As far as I see, all arguments point to the magnitude of being able to do nothing and live well. This notion is what has inspired the following chapter: The Importance of Appearing Busy.

CHAPTER 19

The Importance Of Appearing Busy

Looking busy is most important while at work. Or when you are home, and you're pretending in front of your spouse or respective partner that you're being productive. Rarely do pets, roommates or friends care if you are motivated. Otherwise, you never have to look busy, unless of course, you're avoiding a potential snag. (Refer back to Chapter 8.)

As far as work goes, I'm addressing this topic to the unfortunate people who work for someone else. It's the majority of us, so don't feel too badly. If you own your own business, enterprise, company, building, corporation, restaurant, or if you employ anyone at all – do not read this! This advice does not apply to you. However, if you are in charge of overseeing others in any capacity, yet are under close scrutiny yourself, then you might want to pay attention to this section.

By now, many of you have reformed to my way of thinking and are content to reap the benefits of living life to its fullest. Spending time among friends and family, eating and drinking merrily, and having a lot of sex are now your top priorities. Caught in the moment, you're probably ignoring all of your responsibilities. This is positive behavior. Enjoying yourself will continue to provide further relaxation.

Nevertheless, most of us still have to work. At work, we must appear busy as to not draw attention to ourselves. Giving the impression of being busy is also important because being fired is a pain in the ass. It's a huge relief at first, but then finding another job always requires effort, without compensation.

Just to be clear, *looking* busy is different than *being* busy. Acting engrossed in your duties is simpler than actually laboring away. After all, it's just an act. This way, if a manager or higher-up is trying to catch you goofing off – they won't succeed. The joke is on them.

Looking busy was a requirement for most of the jobs I've had. My first "real" job was during my high school years. I cooked burgers and cheesesteaks at a local shack masquerading as a franchise of sorts. As I mentioned in the last chapter, half the sales of undercooked hot dogs and pork rolls went in the register, and the other half went into the tip jar. You can imagine how hard it must have been for them to get good workers in 1989; they let me handle money and cook for the public!

In the summer months, when the joint was actually busy, I appeared busy because I was. But here's the deal: when it would slow down the remaining nine months of the year, I still had to look busy! I never understood that. How could I be hard at work if I had nothing to cook and no customers to make fun of? You're either busy or you're not. I could only clean the grill so many times. Why pretend? But then I quickly realized why. In this particular case, it was because if my co-workers and I were just standing around, the proprietor would corner us and start lecturing us on metaphysics. The crazy owner read one Shirley MacLaine book and turned into a fanatic believer in reincarnation overnight. I learned early on that looking busy is your biggest weapon against the boss-snag.

One hopeless day in mid-September, I took apart the hot dog machine on the pretense of cleaning it – just for the sake of looking absorbed in a project. Putting it back together was utterly impossible. My existential boss had to call a mechanic to reassemble it. After that day, the contraption never rolled those footlong dogs the same.

My point is this: despite the additional cost to the root beer stand, disassembling a mechanism I knew nothing about preserved my sanity for the evening. I seemed busy and it saved me from having to hear how I might have been a butterfly in a past life. It was worth every bit of the trouble I caused.

I probably have a story for every place I have ever worked, but to recount them all would take forever. This is another one, however, that stands out in my mind:

Sidebar: I was at Flask one hauntingly slow night and there was only one customer upstairs in the "Blue Room." And he, Jim, happened to be a friend of mine who I'd called to come over and keep me company. I sat down with him and helped him eat his duck salad. We drank champagne and discussed our favorite writers. Forgetting to be on the lookout, I lit a cigarette and leaned back in my chair.

At that moment, the overzealous and extremely pretentious owner of Flask decided to check who was in the Blue Room. His official name was René, but I referred to him as Frenchie. He spotted me just as I took a drag off my Marlboro, holding my champagne up to my lips. When I looked up, it was too late. I mean, I could have chucked both objects behind me, but I rather doubt that would have scored me any last minute points. Broken glass and fires tend not to improve an already bad situation.

So instead, I remained in my seat and motioned him over to the table like I was about to host the dinner party of the year. He looked skeptical, but I didn't care. I acted nonchalant and introduced Frenchie to Jim. The introduction was beyond forced. I made up some shit about Jim potentially promoting the bar. I'm sure I sounded stupid, but it was worth a shot.

If you're ever caught doing nothing, it's always best to just keep quiet. Apologizing rarely works either. It just brings more attention to you. Frenchie acted polite and then swiftly wrote me up—like I cared. But you get the point. He eventually fired me, but I hung on by a thin thread for months longer than I thought I would by pretending to be busy after Frenchie caught me chilling with Jim.

An important rule in appearing busy is remembering our prior mistakes. For instance, at the shack, I never took the hot dog machine apart again. I chose less-challenging appliances to screw with. I would lightly sponge off the ice cream machine or slowly stir the fake cheese sauce. At Flask, I began smoking where I could keep an eye on the people coming upstairs. (I was not fired for smoking!)

An important aspect of looking busy entails learning what your actual job description is. That's always a bitch, but necessary, since "faking" your job is just as effective as doing it. You only need a general job description; the details rarely matter. If a manager or customer asks you anything specific, you can always invent an answer, or simply circle around it. Or just say yes. For instance:

"Amy, did you polish the silverware?"

"You bet!"

It's really very simple. And the more outgoing you seem about something you didn't know you were supposed to do, the better. People in charge love enthusiasm! Humor them; they will be thrilled.

When asked a stupid question by a foolhardy customer: *"How's the lamb chop prepared?"* Instead of saying what you're actually thinking, *You dumb fuck, how many different ways are there to cook a lamb chop?* Keep it simple. I used to just answer back, *However you'd like it.* This response put the pressure back on them, and nine times out of ten, they panicked and said, "I trust the chef." I never even had to know how things were prepared. Being nonspecific tends to be your best bet when you have no idea what the answer is.

Speaking of researching your current or potential job beforehand reminds me of the time I thought I might try my hand at being a temp at a firm in the Condé Nast building in Manhattan. I actually did a little investigating of what was expected of me, and it wasn't good. It involved typing eighty words a minute, answering the phone properly and filing documents. I typed with one finger, I didn't realize there was a right and a wrong way to answer the phone, and I was unclear what "filing" really entailed. I didn't even know how to fake it. At any rate, obtaining basic criteria is essential when it comes to doing the absolute minimum. In this particular case, I saved myself the time and energy of the application process, possibly interviewing, and, ultimately, being rejected.

Another good way to act busy on the spot can be orchestrated through something as simple as your expression. Looking serious is key. If you appear to be concentrating, employers assume you care. Like you're *determined* to think of the catchiest slogan or the freshest new graphics. For instance, in my world at Flask, I'd often act like I was studying the extensive champagne list for better selling knowledge, when really, I was simply deciding what to drink next.

A truly solemn expression can also distract your employer, making them think there is no way in hell you're goofing off or having any fun. Looking a little angry works too. As if something job-related has gone awry, and it's up to you to save the day. Your face should be one of intense determination, a signal to everyone that you are in charge.

Whenever Frenchie used to close in on me, my expression would automatically transform from a careless eye roll to one of deep focus. I'd even feel my eyebrows furrow inward. I remember clenching my jaw and converting my light, bouncy stroll into a swift, powerful stride. This performance signified two things:

1) Don't talk to me.

2) I'm extremely busy.

Consequently, I'm sure I appeared too busy. The arrival of Queen Elizabeth would have been the only reason to look so on top of things. And it doesn't matter where you're heading as long as you are marching by quickly. I once practically sprinted by Frenchie, just to finish my half-eaten McDonald's sundae in the back station, the fear of it melting my only incentive. It's how you *appear* that matters. If you don't look busy at work, you're just asking for trouble.

One of my best tricks was acting like I was always in a hurry. My coworkers used to say to each other, "Look at Amy. She's doing the conspicuous hustle again." It didn't matter if I was just heading to the bathroom, if Frenchie was in the vicinity, I was suddenly racing across the restaurant floor.

I worked at a café on Fifty-seventh Street for many years. The Greek owners were constantly hiring and firing managers, but the one who lasted the longest was the one who was always rushing around. He repeatedly had to cut the staff meetings short because there was always a more important meeting to go to. And if he was in the office with his feet up just staring into space, he was "actively" waiting for an important phone call from the boss. I still have tremendous respect for that guy. He really had the act down pat.

The hardest face for me to master is the *I'm paying close attention* face. I blink too many times, and I resemble a deer trapped in headlights. Feigning listening is a true talent. I've never been good at it. (My husband can confirm this.) The daily staff meetings at the plethora of restaurants I worked used to put me over the edge. I never absorbed a word. Frenchie used to drone on and on about the fermentation of champagne, and I had absolutely no idea what he was talking about. *Something about monks in a cave? Why was this important?* It wasn't like our customers were there to learn about the distilling process. Half our clientele had to hold one hand over an eye in order to read the label on the bottle they'd selected at random.

To this day, if I'm forced to listen to a lecture, I glare at the speaker intently, striving to make him or her uncomfortable. This gives the impression I care, while I strategize where to eat my next meal.

I've never had a real desk job so I can't elaborate on how to appear busy in corporate America. I would imagine the only good thing about having an "official" job – as in nine to five – is that, more times than not, you're sitting at a desk attached to a computer. You can appear busy while you're playing online poker – providing they haven't blocked anything fun on your server, which is sadly often the case. Desks also have plenty of hiding spots for portable electronic games, crossword puzzles, comic books, magazines and other imperative reading material.

It wasn't actually that long ago that I took a job in retail at my local mall here in Florida. I was doing some research for a character in a novel I was working on. The only prior time I had ever worked retail, was for three weeks when I was fifteen, and boy did I suddenly remember how to pretend to look busy again! It was like all my tricks came flooding back to me and I was still a kid folding the same brown sweater over and over again.

Almost thirty years later, my short-lived retail experience happened to be at a skincare store. Despite selling face cream as opposed to designer clothing to senior citizens, the politics were frighteningly the same: if my boss was looking at me, appearing busy was crucial! When she was present, I immediately began straightening the rows of fancy soap or spritzing lavender fragrance into the air. I rather doubt

I fooled her on any level as she was quite sharp, but I did my best to pretend I liked the job. I would even approach the customers when she was lurking nearby, but that often backfired. One day a woman wearing a large frilly hat was sampling from a spray can of "cooling mist." She asked me if the mist would stay cool in her golf bag on warm days and I reminded her that most children in Africa still have to walk five miles in the desert to a stream or river to procure clean drinking water. I'm not much of a salesperson, but I believe I effectively made my point.

That didn't go over very well with my boss. Always listening, she stepped in front of me, shoeing me away like a fly, which was fine with me. I caught up on my text messages and ate the rest of my Thai crunch salad from California Pizza Kitchen. The bottom line is even though I didn't sell the shit out of the "cooling mist," I did not appear idle, and that in itself is commendable.

Sidebar #2: Many years have passed since I worked at Fashion Café in 1995. For a restaurant, that was a dangerously corporate environment. The management discouraged any downtime whatsoever.

I flew into work every day a little after 10 a.m. The obnoxious, fame-obsessed tourists hoping to catch a glimpse of Naomi Campbell didn't begin arriving until noon, so the other waiters and I would hang out in this large side-station, doing various side work (a.k.a. busywork.) I usually opted to fill the salt and pepper shakers, always sliding a set in my bag for home use. Otherwise, I stocked the sugar caddies. *Same idea.*

Anyway, one day during those couple of hours, I was getting lax with my self-imposed strategies of appearing busy, and I was reading Page Six of *The New York Post*. This is why I didn't notice my general manager, Bruce, staring at me from across the room. He had a creepy ghost-like ability to appear out of nowhere, and I'd forgotten he was working that day. Trite and corny, Bruce spent most of his time trying to prove his authority to me and the other out-of-work actors who barely noticed him.

"What am I thinking right now?" Bruce said to me.

I slowly lowered my paper and glanced around. Everyone else looked convincingly busy. I shifted my gaze back to him. "Umm . . . you're wondering why you have so many servers scheduled for a Monday lunch?"

"No. Funny, though. Try again."

I stared at his stupid Fashion Café cap. He was the only one to wear the ridiculous items sold in the gift shop. "Maybe you're wondering why four supermodels run your life?"

"No, but maybe I should wonder."

At this point all my friends had turned to watch us. "I give up," I said. "Perhaps you're wishing you'd brought your own newspaper to work."

"Close."

The realization set in. "Are you sending me home?"

"Bingo." He grinned.

"Just because I didn't look busy enough?" I hollered. I was so mad that I jumped up too quickly and slipped into the garbage can, knocking it over. To wake up any time before 10 a.m. for absolutely no reason was just about the worst thing that could happen to me back then. Living day-to-day, it also meant I had no cash for happy hour. Soon after I'd quit that stupid job, I was thrilled to learn that the primary owners of Fashion Café were sitting in jail for money laundering and fraud, which meant Bruce was most likely reading *The Post* on a park bench in Central Park.

Just to reiterate, the stricter the environment, the greater the need to look busy. Skye, my friend and co-worker at Fashion Café, spent her spare time with a video camera taping the shenanigans of the staff, under the guise of "free publicity." She managed to capture a couple of good, solid restaurant violations on film. She later used these tapes as security for her job. That's what I should have been doing in the mornings instead of reading gossip columns and downing Long Island Ice Teas with the dishwasher.

Acting impatient is another great way to look busy. Stare at the ceiling and quickly tap your foot. Then glance at your watch, look away dramatically, and sigh deeply.

It doesn't matter what you're pretending to be waiting for, as long as you look annoyed by its late arrival. Whether it's the Chinese food you ordered or a document that's critical to completing your work task, you must act as its appearance must occur before anything else can be accomplished. If you're waiting for absolutely nothing (as usual), then have something ready to say in case you're asked.

I always have an excuse ready. Back when I was tending

bar, my standard line was, "Where the fuck is the barback? I can't do anything until he gets here!" In theory, my impatience stemmed from inadequate working conditions and the actual job, which required speaking to customers, so my irritation was highly believable.

Compliments, and/or unabashed flattery, also work well when distracting supervisors from your indolent behavior. "God, you look nice today!" is one of my favorites. It turns the attention back on the enemy. It makes him or her wonder if their new diet is working, or if something else they're doing to spruce up their look is finally taking effect. "That color looks great on you!" is another gem. "Brings out your eyes!" (You'd be surprised how unoriginal catch phrases still manage to effectively distract.) Frenchie always wore this high-collared dark gray sports jacket. Combined with his sallow eyes and pale complexion, the color made him appear two steps away from death, and he still wanted to believe me when I complimented him.

It is a known fact that compliments and praise boost people's confidence. Be sure to use direct eye contact when flattering as you will seem more convincing. He or she might even walk away thinking how truly perceptive you are. Don't count on it, but you never know.

I had this manager once who couldn't dress to save her life. I mean, I'm no fashionista, but this woman was donning random articles of clothing and haphazardly placing them on her various body parts. She was basically dressing for a multitude of different functions at the same time. One day, I walked past her and noticed she was wearing red fleece sweat pants, a gold sequin top, shiny black tap shoes from another era, and a bright pink wool scarf. It was August in NYC. I'll never forget the image as long as I live. Her name was Dina, but I called her Disco from day one. When she first interviewed me for the job, she was wearing silver velvet bell-bottomed pants and I couldn't look away.

I struggled to think of a compliment I could throw at her, and settled for "That's a jazzy blouse."

"Amy, your attempt at flattery won't work on me. I need you to greet table nine, and table four still doesn't have their drinks."

"Too bad it looks ridiculous with the rest of your outfit," I added.

Disco fired me on the spot, but the good news was I didn't have to greet table nine. I went straight to the service bar and poured table four's two glasses of merlot into a Styrofoam cup, making myself a drink to go. As it turned out, Disco was not just a bizarre dresser, but also a bit of an idiot. She fired me in the middle of a shift forgetting the cash sales for the day were still in my possession.

The moral of this little tale is if flattery doesn't work, remember to keep your cool. If people in charge tell you to do something, the answer is always, "Yes, yes, and yes." (Learn from my mistakes.) Yes them to death. You don't have to do a single thing – remember that. If they *think* you're doing it, that's all that matters.

Many managers, supervisors, and owners act suspicious when you say nice things. These people are smarter and more intelligent because they have been around the block. Minimal interaction with them is best at all times. Better yet, avoid them at all costs. If you see them heading in your direction, go the other way. The less you interact, the longer you'll stay employed.

On another note, being too friendly with the boss always backfires. He or she winds up either owing you money or hitting on you. They either won't trust you, with good reason, or they get the wrong idea. It's better just to act busy.

My overall advice: try to get into the habit of looking busy. Practice turning it on and off. It should be reserved solely for when a higher-up is watching you, whether they are in the same room or sitting in the office staring at you through the camera. Eventually, you'll get so good at improvising, auto-pilot will kick in, saving you from aggravating consequences.

Good luck avoiding all forms of work!

CHAPTER 20

Doing Nothing In 2020

There is no better way to end this book. Unfortunately, doing nothing really took on new meaning for everyone in year 2020. This was not a positive experience for the majority of us.

I'm going to go month by month from my perspective in order to give you a vivid picture of how quickly a culture can be impacted in so many ways.

January

In the beginning of the year, I was still carrying on in my normal delusional fashion, engaging in everything fun that I took for granted. Obviously, this was mostly partaking in the four exceptions to the rules: eating, drinking, smoking, and having sex. I was also enjoying my morning spin class followed by lunch out at various restaurants around town, where I was beginning to formulate this book using my laptop. And, above all, I was mingling every evening in some capacity. In South Florida, January kicks off the high social season. There are nightly Palm Beach events, fundraisers and gatherings, with many having hundreds in attendance.

However, even globally in the news there was chatter. Something unclear had gone awry in China resulting in an unknown airborne virus. Most of us in South Florida really didn't pay much attention, despite the fact that the World Health Organization (WHO) had issued a global health emergency by the end of the month.

Not always particularly news orientated, preferring to read about entertaining current events, this infectious disease affecting Asia was oddly something to which I actually paid attention. I had a bad feeling. I remember expressing my concern to my husband, Ron, who assured me this virus was contained in Asia and would not impact America. I do not know why I ever listen to him, but it was easier to believe him then to worry about it. I continued to prioritize my doing nothing principals and engage in the four exceptions to the rules.

February

On February 2, the majority of the U.S. was enjoying watching the Kansas City Chiefs beat the San Francisco 49ers in the Super Bowl. The football party I attended was a small one – perhaps thirty people. Keep in mind, Hard Rock Stadium in Miami, where the game was played, can pack as many as 65,000-plus spectators, and that day was no exception.

The Trump Administration waited until the following day to declare a public health emergency due to the rising cases of the coronavirus in the U.S. and confirmed deaths all over the world. Now people were talking, but again, those of us in South Florida were still carrying on as usual. I knew better than to ask Ron's opinion, not that it mattered; I was privy to his unsolicited online news bulletins every time I turned around.

March

In early March, while cases and deaths from this new disease, now named COVID-19 (also known as coronavirus) were rising all over the world, Ron and I attended a charity benefit in West Palm Beach. Over 200 donors were all packed into one large room. There were no masks or precautions, only a detectable wave of fear spreading through the room as we drank our champagne and ate crudités asking each other if we should all really be there. By this point, New York and California had shut down completely. We drank our champagne faster, gobbling our dinners and concealing our fears. *Should we have postponed this event? Are we not being socially conscious?* The answer was yes, the event should have been postponed, and we were all irresponsible fools.

The middle of March was when the "shit (officially) hit the fan" in South Florida. On March 11, a man wearing a mask and gloves who had just tested positive for coronavirus boarded a JetBlue flight from JFK in New York to PBI airport in West Palm Beach, potentially exposing both airports and an entire plane to the virus. Despite this, Florida officials released all passengers without requiring isolation or testing. That was when I knew we were done for. Hearing that, Ron and I decided we were homebound indefinitely. By March 31, *Our World in Data* reported there were 3,170 deaths and 164,620 confirmed cases of COVID-19 in the U.S. For the first time in my history, it was actually dangerous NOT to do nothing.

April-July

On April 1, Florida Governor, Ron DeSantis, implemented a stay-at-home order throughout the state of Florida. I will always remember the months of April and May of 2020 as ones of utter helplessness and daunting uncertainty. The majority of those who were lucky enough to keep their jobs were forced to work remotely. Thousands of people were out of a job with no guarantee of returning to it in the near future, or possibly ever.

It is one thing to inspire to "do nothing." It is another thing entirely to be told you have to. And here I was writing a book about the joys of goofing off. Well, obviously, my book now required total restructuring. The world was now suddenly a different place, and my personal experiences could no longer be current day examples. I resorted back to happier times from my past in order to effectively convey my points.

As each day passed, the pandemic was slowly changing my thinking. Even more so than living through 9/11. My whole life, I was someone who always had a backup plan. I'd been an independent thinker, taking risks, but knowing I could always go back to working in the service industry. But suddenly that security was pulled out from under me. Watching many of my good friends forced to go on unemployment really opened my eyes to the fact that nothing is ever definite. Sometimes you have to acclimate to your current situation in order to survive and be of help to others.

I was also used to working from outside my home, but

I was fortunate in the sense that I can write from anywhere. Easier said than done, naturally. Especially since Ron was working from home too. So on top of the overall sense of unease and doom, I was also subject to his explosions every time the printer or scanner would act up. In this unmoored limbo, my concentration was poor, and I spent most days in the backyard, building unhealthy addictions to social media and online poker. Looking back, I can admit, I was beginning to lose it a little bit. Some of the things I began doing to keep myself and others amused during the pandemic were really bizarre. It was like I was driven to distraction, hoping to relieve the tension that I, and certainly others, were feeling.

By mid-May, I was "starring" in my own live Facebook music videos which I convinced Ron to film to the best of his cinematography ability. At 46 years of age, once a week, I pretended to be a different recording artist in various get-ups, dancing all over my house for the public and my Facebook following.

I also knew I was unraveling because I added cooking videos to my repertoire. I don't know how to cook (refer back to Chapter 7), so the videos were simply expressions of admitting this on camera while staring at a bunch of ingredients. At one point, I juggled black olives before pitching them into a salad bowl like one playing the ring game at a carnival.

I actually attempted cooking, in general, for the first time in my life, but most nights Ron and I simply stared at each other over numerous takeout cardboard boxes. Since Florida doesn't have any decent Chinese food, Thai became our default choice of cuisine.

I will say, if it weren't for the pandemic, I would never have learned about the supermarket. What a fascinating place. As I mentioned, I was strictly a deli shopper in NYC, and in Florida I had only ever run in quickly for such staples as Kraft Singles, Lean Cuisines and numerous packages of chips and Almond Joys.

I also spent a lot of time in my car. Florida had less strict rules than the north so driving aimlessly around, with no destination in mind, was still permitted. Sometimes when you truly have no choice but to do nothing, you find yourself inventing things to do. Most days, I would drive miles to take out my lunch and I'd eat it right in my car. It was strange; the exceptions to the rules were still imperative, but derived out of desperation as opposed to the optimistic freedom to do as I pleased.

August-October

At this point in time, the U.S. was enduring a second wave of the virus, which I was pretty sure was still the first wave. This detail didn't make any difference; the bottom line was people were still getting sick. After six months of captivity, I finally acquired an acceptance of my situation, but I had also concluded that enough was enough. Since outdoor dining in Florida was now allowed, as well as inside dining in Florida – which I avoided, I began to venture out into the world again during the daytime. It felt so good to work from outside my home and continue to support our local restaurants. So my days became more manageable, but my nights . . . well, let's just say I've never watched more TV in my life.

I went on obsessive binges, viewing various unrelated topics. For example, I caught up on my true crime. I saw so many documentaries, that I am now probably qualified to teach a how-to course. There is nothing that I didn't watch or read about. Most people – even under lockdown – could not feasibly watch every true crime documentary and/or re-production that is streaming these days on every imaginable network. I did. I watched Netflix's *The Jeffrey Epstein Story* and *The Disappearance of Madeline McCann* twice, worried I might have missed something. In addition, I'm pretty sure I solved a few "unsolved mysteries" if anyone would just listen to me for longer than twelve seconds.

After I'd exhausted the true crime genre, I found it nec-essary to reacquaint myself with all of Eric Roberts' films go-ing back to the eighties. I attempted to go back farther, but picture quality won out over quantity. I was especially taken with his performance as one of the killers in the made-for-TV movie *In Cold Blood*, circa 1990. Most people are un-aware of how many movies this brilliant actor has actually been in. He is one of the most underrated artists of our time, and I reminded myself of this as I scoured his videography timeline like a crazy person.

I was still somewhat sane at this point, but grateful I had every TV station and streaming app known to man. But here is when I really started to get a little zany. In my true crime blitz, I came across Tori Spelling's awesome performance in *Death of a Cheerleader*. Not only had I crossed paths with it, I was suddenly spellbound by the topic. Cheerleading was an activity I knew nothing about. Granted, my high school experience hadn't helped matters. When I had the misfor-tune to be at one of my high school games, I wondered why these gals were dressed up and waving pom-poms around. It seemed absurd, but then again, at my school, cheerleaders weren't doing pyramids. Nor were they engaging in any interesting gymnastics or choreography for that matter. Nothing that could incite an accident or lawsuit. Just a lot of mindless smiling and high kicks! Why? *These girls weren't getting paid.* I felt badly for them in their heavy blue and white sweaters, pretending we had a chance of winning. My close-knit crowd usually ignored the game. We hung behind the bleachers, smoking cigarettes and drinking anything alcoholic we could get our hands on. Hence, I had never taken cheerleading seriously.

I'd never realized how cheerleading had evolved into such a competitive sport. *I learned so much from the movies I watched!* Therefore, a few details must be recognized and discussed. What I found especially interesting was not one of the movies began with a girl that actually wanted to be a cheerleader. They all asked their mother – in the car, before being cannonballed off to a new school – if there was a dance team. How is that even possible? Dance team? My high school was lucky to have an acceptable gymnasium. But the thread remained the same throughout almost every cheerleading movie. Not only was the mother central to every story, sometimes the movies even used the same theme songs!

On Prime, I watched *Cheerleader Escort, The Secret Lives of Cheerleaders, Cheerleader Identity Theft, Undercover Cheerleader, Cheerleader Camp, Cheerleaders-An American Myth, The Swinging Cheerleaders,* and *All Cheerleaders Die.* Just to name a few. Once I got rolling, I couldn't stop. I went from ignorant to informed, and because I was watching these movies one after the other, it was impossible not to start rating them in my head.

Undercover Cheerleader was really the best. One of the new girls who just joined the team asked when the first football game was, and the coach glared at her and said, "We don't cheer at male-dominated games. We only compete." I was like *Wow! This is fabulous! Undercover Cheerleader* inspired me to finally watch a cheerleading movie that had actually made it to the theaters called *Bring it On*. I sat there watching girls do back flips off the top of a massive human pyramid and realized how stupid I'd been. By the time *Dare Me*, the cheerleading miniseries, came on Netflix, I was able to recognize a good thing right away.

During these few months of binge-watching cable, I realized there were a lot of things I was shortsighted about. Sure, I knew "doing nothing" would always take top priority, but could I use this time while I was really *doing nothing* to learn more? Grow? Expand my horizons, if by only scrutinizing television and reading? Using just my mind, so my body didn't have to be involved? I mean, I was just sitting there anyway. If I could refresh my memory on every true crime reported in the U.S., Spain, Italy, Portugal, Bermuda, Aruba . . . et cetera, while sitting on the couch, flanked on either side by buttered popcorn and Cherry Coke, then certainly I could learn about other topics as well.

November-December

November 28, 2020, the morning after Thanksgiving, I awakened with a deep guttural cough. *No, I have not just spent nine months in captivity in order to get COVID when a vaccine is right around the corner,* I thought. I had lunch plans with a girlfriend that day, but I had the good sense to cancel. I know myself well, and I when I get sick there is a pattern to it. I wake up with a sore throat, then the sniffles follow. The itchy watery eyes and sneezing generally coincide with achiness and general malaise as the sore throat slowly abates. After I've gone through at least five boxes of tissues, I finally get the cough. The cough is LAST. It signifies the cold is ending, not beginning.

So, I knew something was up, and asked the question I'd been asking all year that never yielded an answer. Can one still get sick and *not* have COVID? By the next day I had full blown chills and didn't have wine with dinner – a red flag to anyone who knows me. The chills stayed with me for two days and I didn't leave our TV room. Doctor Ron came in periodically to take my temperature and blood oxygen level, and to assure me I did not have COVID because he felt healthy as a horse.

For such a smart man, I just stared at him, disbelieving how stupid he could be. "You have no fever," he declared with authority.

"I'm not prone to fevers. I'm not even sure I had them often as a kid."

"All kids get fevers."

"Perhaps not me. And there is no way of finding out for sure, as my mother would never remember."

"Amy, you do not have COVID! I feel better than ever."

"Yeah, that's because you like working from home."

At any rate, I also had a slight headache, which added to my skepticism. I never have headaches, and there had been times in my life when people who I've merely tolerated, could have been the cause of plenty.

Then came the stuffy head and the myriad of tissues. Doctor Ron stated with blind conviction, "Of course you can't smell or taste – you have a bad cold."

Skeptical, I put on my strongest perfume – a deep lilac scent that the pelicans perching on the Intracoastal would squawk at – and I couldn't smell it. Nothing. The same night, I was eating a salad and got pissed off because I thought the restaurant we got takeout from gave me creamy Italian instead of ranch. It turned out to be blue cheese. That did it. "Tomorrow morning I'm getting tested for COVID," I declared, putting down my fork. Doctor Ron tried to talk me out of it despite the fact I hadn't drunk any wine all week, but I went anyway. He insisted on driving me in order to say he was right, and I had not been infected. I rolled my eyes and entered the building in order to get a rapid test.

"Positive. I told you," I said, getting back in the car.

He just stared at me blankly while I handed him a sheet of paper with my proof of illness. "It must be a mistake," he said, peering disbelievingly at the paper, but he still divided the house in half when we got home. From literally spending every second together in bed or watching TV (Ron had to endure a few cheerleading flicks with me) the living room suddenly became the common area, in which we were both required to wear masks, as Ron dictated new rules. It was truly the dumbest thing in the world, but I didn't have the energy to fight him on it. It was too cute.

Still unconvinced, despite the new protocol he'd set in place, the following morning Ron dragged me to West Palm Beach at the crack of dawn to get the "more sensitive" test. He pulled a favor and I got my results in three hours as opposed to three days. Negative. Ron was gloating. Smiling from ear to ear. "See, I knew you didn't have it. Rapid tests give false positives all the time," he declared, finally whipping off his mask. I just rolled my eyes, knowing they really didn't. False negatives, maybe.

So I settled back into the media room for the next few days, marking the calendar for four weeks from the day. That would be when I would go get tested for the antibodies I was certain to have. And *did* have. And still do.

Ron was vaccinated early on, and I was recently vaccinated and am back to my routine. Spin class in the mornings and then writing *inside* a restaurant during lunch. Except things are not the same. I'm not the same. I'm quieter. I'm stronger. I'm smarter. In conclusion, I'm improved.

A return to really doing nothing in 2021, and for many years to come, is my goal. I hope this book inspires others to do the same, leaving more time for the four exceptions to the rules.